# GASTRIC SLEEVE COOKBOOK

## 3 MANUSCRIPTS

### BARIATRIC COOKBOOK: FLUID

50 Bariatric-Friendly Broth, Beverage, Popsicle and Mousse recipes for Stage I and II Fluid Diets for Post Weight Loss Surgery Recovery

### BARIATRIC COOKBOOK: PUREE

50 Unique Bariatric-Friendly Soup, Puree, Smoothie and Dessert recipes for Stage III and IV Puree and Soft Food Diets for Post Weight Loss Surgery Recovery

### GASTRIC BYPASS COOKBOOK: MAIN COURSE

70+ Bariatric-Friendly Chicken, Beef, Fish, Pork, Fish, Salads and Vegetarian recipes for lifelong eating for Post Weight Loss Surgery Diet

## STELLA LAYNE

# CONTENT

## BARIATRIC COOKBOOK: FLUID

(C) SUITABLE FOR CLEAR FLUID       (F) SUITABLE FOR FULL FLUID

### BROTH/SOUP RECIPES (C) (F)

# BARIATRIC COOKBOOK: PUREE

# SMOOTHIES RECIPES

# DESSERT RECIPES

# GASTRIC BYPASS COOKBOOK: MAIN COURSE

## BEEF RECIPES

## CHICKEN RECIPES

## FISH RECIPES

# SIMPLE SEAWEED SOUP

 **SERVES** 8

 **PREP TIME** 15 MINUTES

 **COOK TIME** 30 MINUTES

- **8 ounces** 97/3 lean ground beef

- **1 ounce** dried brown seaweed

- **2 cloves** garlic, minced

- **5 cups** water

- **1/2 teaspoon** salt

- Nonstick cooking spray

1. Soak the seaweed for 10 minutes. Chop into pieces.

2. Sauté the garlic until fragrant. Then brown the meat.

3. Add water. Bring it to a boil. Then reduce to low heat. Cover and simmer for 15 minutes.

4. Skim off the fat on the surface. Add seaweed. Simmer for another 10 minutes.

5. Remove the solid from the soup. Set aside to cool to room temperature. Refrigerate overnight.

6. Remove the solid layer of fat formed on the surface of the soup.

# BEAN SPROUT
## AND PORK SPARERIB SOUP

 **SERVES** 4

 **PREP TIME** 10 MINUTES

 **COOK TIME** 50 MINUTES

1. In a medium pot, add 3-4 cups of water. Bring it to a boil. Blanch the pork for 5 minutes.

2. Discard the water. Rinse the pork to remove surface impurities.

3. Add water, pork, garlic, green onion and ginger to the pot. Bring it to a boil. Then reduce to low heat. Cover and simmer for 30 minutes.

4. Skim off the fat on the surface. Add bean sprouts. Simmer for another 10 minutes.

5. Remove the solid from the soup. Set aside to cool to room temperature. Refrigerate overnight.

6. Remove the solid layer of fat formed on the surface of the soup.

- **12 ounces** extra lean pork spareribs, visible fat trimmed, cut along the ribs

- **6 ounces** bean sprout

- **1** green onion, roughly chopped

- **2 cloves** garlic, minced

- **2 slices** fresh ginger root

- **3 cups** water

- **1/4 teaspoon** salt

- Nonstick cooking spray

# CLASSIC FISH STOCK

 **SERVES**
**12**

 **PREP TIME**
**10**
MINUTES

 **COOK TIME**
**50**
MINUTES

- **1 pound** fish bones from bass, flounder or halibut, cut into pieces and clean off all the blood

- **4 stalks** celery, chopped

- **1** medium onion, peeled and chopped

- **7 cups** water

- **1** bay leave

- **2 tablespoons** chopped fresh parsley

- **2 tablespoons** chopped fresh thyme

- **1 tablespoon** black peppercorns

- **1 teaspoon** salt

**1.** Add water to a large pot. Bring it a boil. Add ginger root and fish bones. Boil over high heat for 10 minutes.

**2.** Add celery and onion. Once boiled, reduce to low heat. Cover and simmer for 40 minutes. Add salt.

**3.** Remove the solid from the soup. Set aside to cool to room temperature. Refrigerate overnight.

**4.** Remove the solid layer of fat formed on the surface of the soup.

# CHICKEN AND BOK CHOY SOUP

 **SERVES** **4**

 **PREP TIME** **10** **MINUTES**

 **COOK TIME** **50** **MINUTES**

1. Add water and chicken to the pot. Bring it to a boil. Then reduce to low heat. Cover and simmer for 40 minutes.

2. Skim off the fat on the surface. Add Bok Choy and green onion. Simmer for another 10 minutes.

3. Remove the solid from the soup. Set aside to cool to room temperature. Refrigerate overnight.

4. Remove the solid layer of fat formed on the surface of the soup.

- **12 ounces** bone-in chicken pieces

- **1/2 pound** baby bok choy

- **1** green onion, roughly chopped

- **3 cups** water

- **1/4 teaspoon** salt

# BEEF SHANK BROTH
## WITH VEGETABLES

 **SERVES**
**12**

 **PREP TIME**
**10**
MINUTES

 **COOK TIME**
**50**
MINUTES

- **1 pound** lean beef shank, visible fat trimmed, diced

- **2** medium carrots, peeled and chopped

- **1/2** medium white radish, peeled and chopped

- **2 slices** fresh ginger root

- **7 cups** water

- **1/2 teaspoon** salt

1. In a large pot, add 3-4 cups of water. Bring it to a boil. Blanch the beef for 5 minutes.

2. Discard the water. Rinse the beef to remove surface impurities.

3. Add water, beef and all vegetables to the pot. Bring it to a boil. Then reduce to low heat. Cover and simmer for 40 minutes.

4. Remove the solid from the soup. Set aside to cool to room temperature. Refrigerate overnight.

5. Remove the solid layer of fat formed on the surface of the soup.

# FISH BROTH
## WITH TOMATO AND TOFU

 **SERVES**
12

 **PREP TIME**
10
MINUTES

 **COOK TIME**
50
MINUTES

1. Add water to a large pot. Bring it a boil. Add ginger root and fish bones. Boil over high heat for 10 minutes.

2. Add tomatoes and tofu. Once boiled, reduce to low heat. Cover and simmer for 40 minutes. Add salt.

3. Remove the solid from the soup. Set aside to cool to room temperature. Refrigerate overnight.

4. Remove the solid layer of fat formed on the surface of the soup.

- **1 pound** fish bones from bass, flounder or halibut, cut into pieces and clean off all the blood

- **2 cups** finely chopped tomatoes

- **1 block** silken tofu, cubed

- **4 slices** fresh ginger root

- **7 cups** water

- **1/2 teaspoon** salt

# BEET AND VEGETABLES
## BONE BROTH

 **SERVES** 8

 **PREP TIME** 15 MINUTES

 **COOK TIME** 75 MINUTES

- **1 pound** beef bones, visible fat trimmed

- **1/2** medium beet root, peeled and chopped

- **1/2** medium onion, peeled and chopped

- **5 cups** water

- **1/4 teaspoon** salt

1. In a large pot, add 3-4 cups of water. Bring it to a boil. Blanch the beef bones for 5 minutes.

2. Discard the water. Rinse the beef to remove surface impurities.

3. Add water and bones to the pot. Bring it to a boil. Then reduce to low heat. Cover and simmer for 40 minutes.

4. Skim off the fat on the surface. Add all vegetables. Simmer for another 30 minutes. Add salt.

5. Remove the solid from the soup. Set aside to cool to room temperature. Refrigerate overnight.

6. Remove the solid layer of fat formed on the surface of the soup.

# FUZZY GOURD
## AND PEA PORK BONE BROTH

SERVES
12

PREP TIME
15
MINUTES

COOK TIME
75
MINUTES

1. Soak the peas and peanuts in water for 15 minutes. At the same time blanch the pork bones in boiling water for 5 minutes.

2. Discard the water. Rinse the pork to remove surface impurities.

3. Add water, bones, peas and peanuts to the pot. Bring it to a boil. Then reduce to low heat. Cover and simmer for 45 minutes.

4. Skim off the fat on the surface. Add gourd. Simmer for another 30 minutes.

5. Remove the solid from the soup. Set aside to cool to room temperature. Refrigerate overnight.

6. Remove the solid layer of fat formed on the surface of the soup.

- **1 pound** pork bones, visible fat trimmed

- **3** medium fuzzy gourd, cut into 1-inch pieces

- **1/2 cup** dried black-eyed peas

- **1/2 cup** peanuts

- **8 cups** water

- **1/2 teaspoon** salt

# LOTUS ROOT
## AND SOY PORK BONE BROTH

 **SERVES**
**12**

 **PREP TIME**
**15**
MINUTES

 **COOK TIME**
**75**
MINUTES

- **1 pound** pork bones, visible fat trimmed

- **3 cups** thinly sliced lotus roots

- **1 cup** soy beans

- **8 cups** water

- **1/2 teaspoon** salt

**1.** Soak the soy beans in water for 15 minutes. At the same time blanch the pork bones in boiling water for 5 minutes.

**2.** Discard the water. Rinse the pork to remove surface impurities.

**3.** Add water, bones and beans to the pot. Bring it to a boil. Then reduce to low heat. Cover and simmer for 75 minutes.

**4.** Remove the solid from the soup. Set aside to cool to room temperature. Refrigerate overnight.

**5.** Remove the solid layer of fat formed on the surface of the soup.

# PAPAYA AND PEANUT
## PORK BONE BROTH

 **SERVES** **12**

 **PREP TIME** **15** MINUTES

 **COOK TIME** **75** MINUTES

1. Soak the peanuts in water for 15 minutes. At the same time blanch the pork bones in boiling water for 5 minutes.

2. Discard the water. Rinse the pork to remove surface impurities.

3. Add water, papaya, bones and peanuts to the pot. Bring it to a boil. Then reduce to low heat. Cover and simmer for 75 minutes. Add salt

4. Remove the solid from the soup. Set aside to cool to room temperature. Refrigerate overnight.

5. Remove the solid layer of fat formed on the surface of the soup.

- **1 pound** pork bones, visible fat trimmed

- **1/2** medium papaya, peeled, seeded and chopped

- **1 cup** peanuts

- **8 cups** water

- **1/2 teaspoon** salt

# TUMERIC AND GINGER
## CHICKEN BROTH

 **SERVES**
**12**

 **PREP TIME**
**15**
MINUTES

 **COOK TIME**
**75**
MINUTES

- **1 pound** bone-in chicken pieces

- **10 shallots**, peeled

- **2** medium carrots, peeled and chopped

- **2 stalks** celery, chopped

- **8 cups** water

- **2 tablespoons** grated fresh ginger root

- **1 tablespoon** ground turmeric

- **1/2 tablespoon** black peppercorns

- **1/2 teaspoon** salt

1. In a large pot, add 3-4 cups of water. Bring it to a boil. Blanch the chicken for 5 minutes.

2. Discard the water. Rinse the Chicken to remove surface impurities.

3. Add water, chicken, spices and all vegetables to the pot. Bring it to a boil. Then reduce to low heat. Cover and simmer for 65 minutes. Add salt

4. Remove the solid from the soup. Set aside to cool to room temperature. Refrigerate overnight.

5. Remove the solid layer of fat formed on the surface of the soup.

# LEMON AND DILL
## CHICKEN SOUP

 **SERVES**
**12**

 **PREP TIME**
**15**
**MINUTES**

 **COOK TIME**
**105**
**MINUTES**

1. In a large pot, add 3-4 cups of water. Bring it to a boil. Blanch the chicken for 5 minutes.

2. Discard the water. Rinse the chicken to remove surface impurities.

3. Sauté the garlic and onion until fragrant. Then add leek and carrot and sauté for another 2-3 minutes.

4. Add all ingredients except dill and salt. Bring it to a boil. Cover and simmer for 90 minutes.

5. Skim off the fat on the surface. Add dill and salt. Simmer for another 10 minutes.

6. Remove the solid from the soup. Set aside to cool to room temperature. Refrigerate overnight.

- **1 pound** bone-in chicken pieces

- **1** medium onion, diced

- **1** medium leek, diced

- **3** medium carrots, diced

- **1** lemon, juice only

- **10 cups** water

- **2 cloves**, garlic minced

- **1** bay leave

- **2 tablespoons** chopped fresh dill

- **1/2 teaspoon** salt

# WATERCRESS
## AND CARROT PORK BONE BROTH

 **SERVES**
**12**

 **PREP TIME**
**15**
**MINUTES**

 **COOK TIME**
**105**
**MINUTES**

- **1 pound** bone-in chicken pieces

- **1 pound** watercress

- **2** carrots, peeled and chopped

- **6** dried red dates, pitted

- **10 cups** water

- **1/2 teaspoon** salt

1. In a large pot, add 3-4 cups of water. Bring it to a boil. Blanch the chicken for 5 minutes.

2. Discard the water. Rinse the chicken to remove surface impurities.

3. Add all ingredients except salt. Bring it to a boil. Cover and simmer for 100 minutes. Add salt

4. Remove the solid from the soup. Set aside to cool to room temperature. Refrigerate overnight.

5. Remove the solid layer of fat formed on the surface of the soup.

# WINTER MELON
## AND COIX SEED BONE BROTH

 **SERVES**
**12**

 **PREP TIME**
**120**
**MINUTES**

 **COOK TIME**
**90**
**MINUTES**

1. Soak the Coix seed in water for 2 hours. Blanch the pork bones in boiling water during the last 5 minutes.

2. Discard the water. Rinse the pork to remove surface impurities.

3. Add water, dates, winter melon and coix seed to the pot. Bring it to a boil. Then reduce to low heat. Cover and simmer for 75 minutes. Add salt

4. Remove the solid from the soup. Set aside to cool to room temperature. Refrigerate overnight.

5. Remove the solid layer of fat formed on the surface of the soup.

- **1 pound** pork bones, visible fat trimmed

- **1 pound** winter melon, cut into 1 inch pieces

- **1 cup** coix seed

- **3** dried red dates, pitted

- **8 cups** water

- **1/2 teaspoon** salt

# GRAPEFRUIT
## AND ROSEMARY WATER

 SERVES
**10**

 PREP TIME
**8**
HOURS

 COOK TIME
**/**
MINUTES

- **4 cups** water

- **1/2** grapefruit, peeled, rind trimmed and sliced

- **1 sprig** fresh rosemary

- liquid stevia to taste

**1.** Add water to a jar container.

**2.** Slowly lower all ingredients except stevia to the container.

**3.** Refrigerate for 8 hours.

**4.** Remove all solid.

**5.** Add liquid stevia to taste before serving if desired.

| CALORIES | CARBS | SUGAR | FAT | PROTEIN | SODIUM |
|---|---|---|---|---|---|
| <10 | <1.0 | <1.0 | <1.0 | <1.0 | <10 |
| KCAL | GRAMS | GRAMS | GRAMS | GRAMS | MILLIGRAMS |

# GREEN TEA WITH CITRUS

 **SERVES**
**10**

 **PREP TIME**
**8**
**HOURS**

 **COOK TIME**
**/**
**MINUTES**

**1.** Add water to a jar container.

**2.** Slowly lower all ingredients except stevia to the container.

**3.** Refrigerate for 4 hours. Remove the tea bags and refrigerate for another 4 hours

**4.** Remove all solid.

**5.** Add liquid stevia to taste before serving if desired.

- **4 cups** water

- **2** decaf green tea bags

- **1** lemon, rind trimmed and sliced

- **1/2 grapefruit**, peeled, rind trimmed and sliced

- liquid stevia to taste

| CALORIES | CARBS | SUGAR | FAT | PROTEIN | SODIUM |
|----------|-------|-------|-----|---------|--------|
| <10 | <1.0 | <1.0 | <1.0 | <1.0 | <10 |
| KCAL | GRAMS | GRAMS | GRAMS | GRAMS | MILLIGRAMS |

# MINTY CUCUMBER
## WATER WITH JALAPEÑO

 **SERVES**
**10**

 **PREP TIME**
**8**
HOURS

 **COOK TIME**
**/**
MINUTES

- **4 cups** water

- **1** medium cucumber, sliced

- **1/2** Jalapeño, de-seeded

- **1 sprig** mint leaves

- liquid stevia to taste

1. Add water to a jar container.

2. Slowly lower all ingredients except stevia to the container.

3. Refrigerate for 8 hours.

4. Remove all solid.

5. Add liquid stevia to taste before serving if desired.

| CALORIES | CARBS | SUGAR | FAT | PROTEIN | SODIUM |
|----------|-------|-------|-----|---------|--------|
| <10 | <1.0 | <1.0 | <1.0 | <1.0 | <10 |
| KCAL | GRAMS | GRAMS | GRAMS | GRAMS | MILLIGRAMS |

# COMBO HERB WATER

 **SERVES**
10

 **PREP TIME**
8
HOURS

 **COOK TIME**
/
MINUTES

1. Add water to a jar container.

2. Slowly lower all ingredients except stevia to the container.

3. Refrigerate for 4 hours. Remove the tea bags and refrigerate for another 4 hours

4. Remove all solid.

5. Add liquid stevia to taste before serving if desired.

- **4 cups** water

- **3** basil leaves

- **2 sprigs** dills

- **1 sprig** lemon thyme

- **1/2 sprig** rosemary

- liquid stevia to taste

| CALORIES | CARBS | SUGAR | FAT | PROTEIN | SODIUM |
|---|---|---|---|---|---|
| <10 | <1.0 | <1.0 | <1.0 | <1.0 | <10 |
| KCAL | GRAMS | GRAMS | GRAMS | GRAMS | MILLIGRAMS |

# LIME AND BLACKBERRY WATER

 **SERVES**
10

 **PREP TIME**
8
HOURS

 **COOK TIME**
/
MINUTES

- **4 cups** water

- **1/2 cup** blackberry, halved

- **1/2** lime, rind removed and sliced

- liquid stevia to taste

1. Add water to a jar container.

2. Slowly lower all ingredients except stevia to the container.

3. Refrigerate for 8 hours.

4. Remove all solid.

5. Add liquid stevia to taste before serving if desired.

| CALORIES | CARBS | SUGAR | FAT | PROTEIN | SODIUM |
|---|---|---|---|---|---|
| <10 | <1.0 | <1.0 | <1.0 | <1.0 | <10 |
| KCAL | GRAMS | GRAMS | GRAMS | GRAMS | MILLIGRAMS |

# LEMONY STRAWBERRY
## AND BASIL WATER

 **SERVES**
**10**

 **PREP TIME**
**8**
HOURS

 **COOK TIME**
**/**
MINUTES

1. Add water to a jar container.

2. Slowly lower all ingredients except stevia to the container.

3. Refrigerate for 4 hours. Remove the tea bags and refrigerate for another 4 hours

4. Remove all solid.

5. Add liquid stevia to taste before serving if desired.

- **4 cups** water

- **4** strawberry, halved

- **1/2** lemon, rind removed and sliced

- **3** basil leaves

- liquid stevia to taste

| CALORIES | CARBS | SUGAR | FAT | PROTEIN | SODIUM |
|----------|-------|-------|-----|---------|--------|
| <10 | <1.0 | <1.0 | <1.0 | <1.0 | <10 |
| KCAL | GRAMS | GRAMS | GRAMS | GRAMS | MILLIGRAMS |

# CILANTRO AND CITRUS WATER

 **SERVES**
**10**

 **PREP TIME**
**8**
HOURS

 **COOK TIME**
/
MINUTES

- **4 cups** water

- **1/2** grapefruit, peeled, rind trimmed and sliced

- **1 sprig** fresh rosemary

- liquid stevia to taste

**1.** Add water to a jar container.

**2.** Slowly lower all ingredients except stevia to the container.

**3.** Refrigerate for 8 hours.

**4.** Remove all solid.

**5.** Add liquid stevia to taste before serving if desired.

| CALORIES | CARBS | SUGAR | FAT | PROTEIN | SODIUM |
|----------|-------|-------|-----|---------|--------|
| <10 | <1.0 | <1.0 | <1.0 | <1.0 | <10 |
| KCAL | GRAMS | GRAMS | GRAMS | GRAMS | MILLIGRAMS |

# RASPBERRY AND ROSE WATER

 SERVES
**10**

 PREP TIME
**8**
HOURS

 COOK TIME
**/**
MINUTES

1. Add water to a jar container.

2. Slowly lower all ingredients except stevia to the container.

3. Refrigerate for 4 hours. Remove the tea bags and refrigerate for another 4 hours

4. Remove all solid.

5. Add liquid stevia to taste before serving if desired.

- **4 cups** water

- **1/2 cup** raspberry, halved

- a handful dried rose petals

- liquid stevia to taste

| CALORIES | CARBS | SUGAR | FAT | PROTEIN | SODIUM |
|----------|-------|-------|-----|---------|--------|
| <10 | <1.0 | <1.0 | <1.0 | <1.0 | <10 |
| KCAL | GRAMS | GRAMS | GRAMS | GRAMS | MILLIGRAMS |

# BLUEBERRY
## AND LAVENDER WATER

 **SERVES**
**10**

 **PREP TIME**
**8**
HOURS

 **COOK TIME**
**/**
MINUTES

- **4 cups** water

- **1/2 cup** blueberry

- **2 sprigs** lavender

- liquid stevia to taste

**1.** Add water to a jar container.

**2.** Slowly lower all ingredients except stevia to the container.

**3.** Refrigerate for 8 hours.

**4.** Remove all solid.

**5.** Add liquid stevia to taste before serving if desired.

| CALORIES | CARBS | SUGAR | FAT | PROTEIN | SODIUM |
|---|---|---|---|---|---|
| <10 | <1.0 | <1.0 | <1.0 | <1.0 | <10 |
| KCAL | GRAMS | GRAMS | GRAMS | GRAMS | MILLIGRAMS |

# LEMON APPLE CIDER VINEGAR WATER

 **SERVES** 10

 **PREP TIME** 8 HOURS

 **COOK TIME** / MINUTES

**1.** Add water to a jar container.

**2.** Slowly lower all ingredients except stevia to the container.

**3.** Refrigerate for 4 hours. Remove the tea bags and refrigerate for another 4 hours

**4.** Remove all solid.

**5.** Add liquid stevia to taste before serving if desired.

- **4 cups** water

- **1/2** lemon, rind removed and sliced

- **2 tablespoons** apple cider vinegar

- liquid stevia to taste

| CALORIES | CARBS | SUGAR | FAT | PROTEIN | SODIUM |
|----------|-------|-------|-----|---------|--------|
| <10 | <1.0 | <1.0 | <1.0 | <1.0 | <10 |
| KCAL | GRAMS | GRAMS | GRAMS | GRAMS | MILLIGRAMS |

# GINGER AND LEMON WATER

**SERVES**
**10**

**PREP TIME**
**8**
HOURS

**COOK TIME**
**/**
MINUTES

- **4 cups** water

- **4 slices** ginger root

- **1/2** lemon, rind removed and sliced

- liquid stevia to taste

**1.** Add water to a jar container.

**2.** Slowly lower all ingredients except stevia to the container.

**3.** Refrigerate for 8 hours.

**4.** Remove all solid.

**5.** Add liquid stevia to taste before serving if desired.

| CALORIES | CARBS | SUGAR | FAT | PROTEIN | SODIUM |
|----------|-------|-------|-----|---------|--------|
| <10 | <1.0 | <1.0 | <1.0 | <1.0 | <10 |
| KCAL | GRAMS | GRAMS | GRAMS | GRAMS | MILLIGRAMS |

# CHOCOLATE COCONUT PARADISE

 **SERVES**
2

 **PREP TIME**
5
MINUTES

 **COOK TIME**
/
MINUTES

**1.** Blend all ingredients until well incorporate

**2.** Add liquid stevia to taste

- **4 ounces** fat-free plain Greek yogurt

- **1/2 cup** unsweetened coconut milk

- **1/2** serving vanilla protein powder

- **1 tablespoon** unsweetened cocoa powder

- **1/4 teaspoon** coconut extract

- liquid stevia to taste

| CALORIES | CARBS | SUGAR | FAT | PROTEIN | SODIUM |
|----------|-------|-------|-----|---------|--------|
| 75 | 5.1 | 1.5 | 2.0 | 10.8 | 62 |
| KCAL | GRAMS | GRAMS | GRAMS | GRAMS | MILLIGRAMS |

# ALMOND JOY SHAKE

**SERVES**
2

**PREP TIME**
5
MINUTES

**COOK TIME**
/
MINUTES

- **3 ounces** fat-free cottage cheese

- **1/2 cup** skim milk

- **1/2 serving** vanilla protein powder

- **2 teaspoons** unsweetened cocoa powder

- **1/4 teaspoon** almond extract

- liquid stevia to taste

**1.** Blend all ingredients until well incorporate

**2.** Add liquid stevia to taste

| CALORIES | CARBS | SUGAR | FAT | PROTEIN | SODIUM |
|----------|-------|-------|-----|---------|--------|
| 92 | 7.4 | 4.4 | 0.7 | 14.5 | 212 |
| KCAL | GRAMS | GRAMS | GRAMS | GRAMS | MILLIGRAMS |

# LEMON CHEESECAKE SMOOTHIE

 **SERVES**
2

 **PREP TIME**
5
MINUTES

 **COOK TIME**
/
MINUTES

1. Blend all ingredients until well incorporate

2. Add liquid stevia to taste

- **3 ounces** fat-free cottage cheese

- **1/2 cup** skim milk

- **1/2 serving** vanilla protein powder

- **1 tablespoon** lemon juice

- liquid stevia to taste

| CALORIES | CARBS | SUGAR | FAT | PROTEIN | SODIUM |
|---|---|---|---|---|---|
| 89 | 6.9 | 4.6 | 0.5 | 13.0 | 211 |
| KCAL | GRAMS | GRAMS | GRAMS | GRAMS | MILLIGRAMS |

# DOUBLE CHOCOLATE DELIGHT

 **SERVES**
2

 **PREP TIME**
5
MINUTES

 **COOK TIME**
/
MINUTES

- **4 ounces** fat-free Greek Yogurt

- **1/2 cup** skim milk

- **1/2 serving** chocolate protein powder

- **1 tablespoon** unsweetened cocoa powder

- **1/4 teaspoon** vanilla extract

- liquid stevia to taste

1. Blend all ingredients until well incorporate

2. Add liquid stevia to taste

| CALORIES | CARBS | SUGAR | FAT | PROTEIN | SODIUM |
|----------|-------|-------|-----|---------|--------|
| 85 | 7.6 | 4.4 | 0.9 | 12.8 | 259 |
| KCAL | GRAMS | GRAMS | GRAMS | GRAMS | MILLIGRAMS |

# PEANUT BUTTER BOMB

 **SERVES** 2

 **PREP TIME** 5 MINUTES

 **COOK TIME** / MINUTES

1. Blend all ingredients until well incorporate

2. Add liquid stevia to taste

- **3 ounces** fat-free plain Greek yogurt

- **1/2 cup** skim milk

- **1/2 serving** vanilla protein powder

- **1 tablespoon** powdered peanut butter

- liquid stevia to taste

| CALORIES | CARBS | SUGAR | FAT | PROTEIN | SODIUM |
|----------|-------|-------|-----|---------|--------|
| 85 | 7.1 | 4.8 | 0.9 | 12.3 | 93 |
| KCAL | GRAMS | GRAMS | GRAMS | GRAMS | MILLIGRAMS |

# LIME AND YOGURT SHAKE

 **SERVES** 2

 **PREP TIME** 5 MINUTES

 **COOK TIME** / MINUTES

- **4 ounces** fat-free plain Greek yogurt

- **1/2 cup** skim milk

- **1/2 serving** vanilla protein powder

- **1 tablespoon** lime juice

- liquid stevia to taste

1. Blend all ingredients until well incorporate

2. Add liquid stevia to taste

| CALORIES | CARBS | SUGAR | FAT | PROTEIN | SODIUM |
|---|---|---|---|---|---|
| 79 | 6.6 | 4.4 | 0.5 | 12.3 | 79 |
| KCAL | GRAMS | GRAMS | GRAMS | GRAMS | MILLIGRAMS |

# GREEN TEA LATTE SHAKE

 **SERVES** 2

 **PREP TIME** 5 MINUTES

 **COOK TIME** / MINUTES

**1.** Blend all ingredients until well incorporate

**2.** Add liquid stevia to taste

- **1/2 cup** skim milk

- **1/4 cup** fat-free half-and-half, whipped

- **1/4 cup** hot water

- **1/2 serving** vanilla protein powder

- **1** decaf green tea bag

- a few ice cubes

- liquid stevia to taste

| CALORIES | CARBS | SUGAR | FAT | PROTEIN | SODIUM |
|----------|-------|-------|-----|---------|--------|
| 75 | 7.1 | 4.7 | 0.9 | 9.3 | 94 |
| KCAL | GRAMS | GRAMS | GRAMS | GRAMS | MILLIGRAMS |

# CHOCOLATE MINT POPSICLE

 **SERVES**
**6**

 **PREP TIME**
**6**
HOURS

 **COOK TIME**
**/**
MINUTES

- **1 cup** fat-free plain Greek yogurt

- **1 1/2 cups** skim milk

- **1 1/2 servings** vanilla protein powder

- **2 tablespoons** unsweetened cocoa powder

- **1/2 teaspoon** Mint Extract

- liquid stevia to taste

**1.** Blend all ingredients until well incorporate

**2.** Add liquid stevia to taste

**3.** Divide the mixture into 6 4-ounce popsicle molds. Insert the sticks. Freeze for 6 hours

| CALORIES | CARBS | SUGAR | FAT | PROTEIN | SODIUM |
|---|---|---|---|---|---|
| 75 | 6.5 | 3.9 | 0.7 | 11.4 | 75 |
| KCAL | GRAMS | GRAMS | GRAMS | GRAMS | MILLIGRAMS |

# PEPPERMINT
## AND CREAM POPSICLES

 **SERVES**
**6**

 **PREP TIME**
**6**
HOURS

 **COOK TIME**
**/**
MINUTES

1. Blend all ingredients until well incorporate

2. Add liquid stevia to taste

3. Divide the mixture into 6 4-ounce popsicle molds. Insert the sticks. Freeze for 6 hours

- **3/4 cup** fat-free half-and-half, slightly whipped

- **1 1/2 cups** skim milk

- **1 1/2 servings** vanilla protein powder

- **3/4 teaspoon** Peppermint Extract

- **1/4 teaspoon** vanilla extract

- liquid stevia to taste

| CALORIES | CARBS | SUGAR | FAT | PROTEIN | SODIUM |
|----------|-------|-------|-----|---------|--------|
| 76 | 7.2 | 4.8 | 0.9 | 9.3 | 95 |
| KCAL | GRAMS | GRAMS | GRAMS | GRAMS | MILLIGRAMS |

# CHOCOLATE TOFU POPSICLE

**SERVES**

**6**

**PREP TIME**

**6**

HOURS

**COOK TIME**

**/**

MINUTES

- **12 ounces** silken tofu

- **1 cup** skim milk

- **1 1/2 servings** vanilla protein powder

- **2 tablespoons** unsweetened cocoa powder

- liquid stevia to taste

**1.** Blend all ingredients until well incorporate

**2.** Add liquid stevia to taste

**3.** Divide the mixture into 6 4-ounce popsicle molds. Insert the sticks. Freeze for 6 hours

| CALORIES | CARBS | SUGAR | FAT | PROTEIN | SODIUM |
|----------|-------|-------|-----|---------|--------|
| 97 | 6.0 | 2.4 | 2.7 | 13.0 | 56 |
| KCAL | GRAMS | GRAMS | GRAMS | GRAMS | MILLIGRAMS |

# PEANUT BUTTER
## AND JELLY POPSICLES

 **SERVES**
6

 **PREP TIME**
6
HOURS

 **COOK TIME**
/
MINUTES

1. Blend all ingredients except Jello until well incorporate

2. Add liquid stevia to taste

3. Stir in the Jello

4. Divide the mixture into 6 4-ounce popsicle molds. Insert the sticks. Freeze for 6 hours

- **2 cups** skim milk

- **3 ounces** sugar-free Jell-O, chopped

- **1 1/2 servings** vanilla protein powder

- **2 tablespoons** powdered peanut butter

- liquid stevia to taste

| CALORIES | CARBS | SUGAR | FAT | PROTEIN | SODIUM |
|----------|-------|-------|-----|---------|--------|
| 73 | 6.4 | 4.7 | 0.8 | 10.0 | 95 |
| KCAL | GRAMS | GRAMS | GRAMS | GRAMS | MILLIGRAMS |

# VANILLA GREEN TEA POPSICLE

**SERVES**
6

**PREP TIME**
6
HOURS

**COOK TIME**
/
MINUTES

- **1 cup** fat-free plain Greek Yogurt

- **1 cup** skim milk

- **1/2 cup** hot water

- **1 1/2 servings** vanilla protein powder

- **1/2 teaspoon** vanilla extract

- **1** decaf green tea bag

- a few ice cubes

- liquid stevia to taste

**1.** Brew the Green tea in the hot water for 5 minutes. Remove the tea bag and cool the tea in ice bath.

**2.** Blend all ingredients until well incorporate

**3.** Add liquid stevia to taste

**4.** Divide the mixture into 6 4-ounce popsicle molds. Insert the sticks. Freeze for 6 hours

| CALORIES | CARBS | SUGAR | FAT | PROTEIN | SODIUM |
|----------|-------|-------|-----|---------|--------|
| 65 | 4.6 | 3.0 | 0.5 | 10.3 | 65 |
| KCAL | GRAMS | GRAMS | GRAMS | GRAMS | MILLIGRAMS |

# GOLDEN TURMERIC
## AND GINGER POPSICLES

 **SERVES**
**6**

 **PREP TIME**
**6.5**
HOURS

 **COOK TIME**
**/**
MINUTES

**1.** In a saucepan, simmer milk with turmeric and ginger for 5 minutes. Remove from heat. Allow to cool for 20 minutes. Carefully remove all solid.

**2.** Blend all ingredients until well incorporate

**3.** Add liquid stevia to taste

**4.** Divide the mixture into 6 4-ounce popsicle molds. Insert the sticks. Freeze for 6 hours

- **3/4 cup** fat-free half-and-half, slightly whipped

- **1 1/2 cups** skim milk

- **1 1/2 servings** vanilla protein powder

- **4 slices** fresh turmeric

- **4 slices** fresh ginger

- liquid stevia to taste

| CALORIES | CARBS | SUGAR | FAT | PROTEIN | SODIUM |
|---|---|---|---|---|---|
| 75 | 7.2 | 4.8 | 0.9 | 9.3 | 95 |
| KCAL | GRAMS | GRAMS | GRAMS | GRAMS | MILLIGRAMS |

# SNICKERDOODLE POPSICLE

 **SERVES**
6

 **PREP TIME**
8
HOURS

 **COOK TIME**
/
MINUTES

- **1 cup** fat-free plain Greek yogurt

- **1 1/2 cups** skim milk

- **1 stick** cinnamon

- **1 1/2 servings** vanilla protein powder

- **1/2 teaspoon** vanilla extract

- **1/2 teaspoon** butter Extract

- Liquid stevia to taste

**1.** Soak the cinnamon stick in the milk for 2 hours. Carefully remove all solid.

**2.** Blend all ingredients until well incorporate

**3.** Add stevia to taste

**4.** Divide the mixture into 6 4-ounce popsicle molds. Insert the sticks. Freeze for 6 hours

| CALORIES | CARBS | SUGAR | FAT | PROTEIN | SODIUM |
|---|---|---|---|---|---|
| 72 | 5.5 | 4.0 | 0.5 | 11.0 | 74 |
| KCAL | GRAMS | GRAMS | GRAMS | GRAMS | MILLIGRAMS |

# BUCKEYE YOGURT MOUSSE

 **SERVES**
4

 **PREP TIME**
5
MINUTES

 **COOK TIME**
/
MINUTES

**1.** Divide the yogurt and protein power in 2 small bowl.

**2.** Stir in the cocoa powder and peanut butter powder respectively. Combine until well incorporated. Add stevia to taste

**3.** Divide the peanut butter mixture into 4 3-ounce mousse cups. Then top with the chocolate mixture.

- **1 1/2 cups** fat-free Greek yogurt

- **1 tablespoon** unsweetened cocoa powder

- **1 tablespoon** powdered peanut butter

- **3/4 serving** vanilla protein powder

- liquid stevia to taste

| CALORIES | CARBS | SUGAR | FAT | PROTEIN | SODIUM |
|----------|-------|-------|-----|---------|--------|
| 67 | 5.1 | 2.3 | 0.7 | 11.3 | 58 |
| KCAL | GRAMS | GRAMS | GRAMS | GRAMS | MILLIGRAMS |

# MOCHA MOUSSE

 **SERVES**
4

 **PREP TIME**
5
MINUTES

 **COOK TIME**
5
MINUTES

- **1 1/2 cups** fat-free Greek yogurt

- **2 tablespoons** skim milk

- **1 tablespoon** unsweetened cocoa powder

- **1 teaspoon** decaf instant coffee crystal

- **3/4 serving** vanilla protein powder

- liquid stevia to taste

**1.** Warm the skim milk. Dissolve the coffee crystal.

**2.** Blend all ingredients until well incorporate

**3.** Add liquid stevia to taste

**4.** Divide the mixture into 4 3-ounce mousse cups and serve.

| CALORIES | CARBS | SUGAR | FAT | PROTEIN | SODIUM |
|---|---|---|---|---|---|
| 64 | 4.7 | 2.2 | 0.6 | 11.0 | 53 |
| KCAL | GRAMS | GRAMS | GRAMS | GRAMS | MILLIGRAMS |

# LEMON YOGURT MOUSSE

 **SERVES**
4

 **PREP TIME**
5
MINUTES

 **COOK TIME**
5
MINUTES

1. Blend all ingredients until well incorporate

2. Add liquid stevia to taste

3. Divide the mixture into 4 3-ounce mousse cups and serve.

- **1 1/2 cups** fat-free Greek yogurt

- **1 tablespoon** lemon juice

- **3/4 serving** vanilla protein powder

- liquid stevia to taste

| CALORIES | CARBS | SUGAR | FAT | PROTEIN | SODIUM |
|----------|-------|-------|-----|---------|--------|
| 59 | 3.8 | 2.0 | 0.4 | 10.5 | 49 |
| KCAL | GRAMS | GRAMS | GRAMS | GRAMS | MILLIGRAMS |

# CINGER MILK CURD

**SERVES**
**4**

**PREP TIME**
**5**
MINUTES

**COOK TIME**
**15**
MINUTES

- **1 1/2 cups** skim milk

- **2 tablespoons** fresh ginger juice

- **1 serving** vanilla protein powder

- liquid stevia to taste

**1.** Divide the ginger juice into 4 3-ounce mousse cups.

**2.** Warm the milk to exactly 150°F. Stir in protein powder. Add liquid stevia to taste.

**3.** Pour the milk from height to the mousse cups in one go. Do not stir afterwards. Allow the mixture to set in room temperature for about 10 minutes before serving.

| CALORIES | CARBS | SUGAR | FAT | PROTEIN | SODIUM |
|----------|-------|-------|-----|---------|--------|
| 69 | 6.2 | 4.8 | 0.5 | 9.5 | 79 |
| KCAL | GRAMS | GRAMS | GRAMS | GRAMS | MILLIGRAMS |

# BLACK FORREST MOUSSE

 **SERVES**
4

 **PREP TIME**
130
MINUTES

 **COOK TIME**
/
MINUTES

1. Soak the gelatin in cherry juice for 10 minutes.

2. Warm the gelatin mixture. Stir until gelatin melts.

3. Blend all ingredients until well incorporate

4. Add liquid stevia to taste

5. Divide the mixture into 4 3-ounce mousse cups. Refrigerate for 2 hours.

- **1 cup** skim milk

- **1/4 cup** no-sugar added/fresh cherry juice

- **1 tablespoon** unsweetened cocoa powder

- **1 serving** vanilla protein powder

- **1 teaspoon** unflavored gelatin powder

- liquid stevia to taste

| CALORIES | CARBS | SUGAR | FAT | PROTEIN | SODIUM |
|---|---|---|---|---|---|
| 70 | 6.8 | 4.7 | 0.7 | 9.5 | 67 |
| KCAL | GRAMS | GRAMS | GRAMS | GRAMS | MILLIGRAMS |

# NEW YORK CHEESECAKE
## MOUSSE

 **SERVES**
**6**

 **PREP TIME**
**130**
MINUTES

 **COOK TIME**
**/**
MINUTES

- **4 ounces** fat-free cream cheese

- **1/2 cup** fat-free half-and-half, whipped

- **1 1/2 servings** vanilla protein powder

- **1 tablespoon** lemon juice

- **1/2 teaspoon** vanilla extract

- liquid stevia to taste

**1.** In a large bowl, whip the cream to form soft peaks

**2.** In another bowl, beat the cheese with lemon juice until fluffy. Add protein powder and mix until well incorporated.

**3.** Fold in whipped cream. Add stevia to taste.

**4.** Divide the mixture into 6 3-ounce mousse cups. Refrigerate for 2 hours.

| CALORIES | CARBS | SUGAR | FAT | PROTEIN | SODIUM |
|----------|-------|-------|-----|---------|--------|
| 69 | 5.1 | 2.6 | 1.0 | 10.0 | 190 |
| KCAL | GRAMS | GRAMS | GRAMS | GRAMS | MILLIGRAMS |

# SIMPLE COCONUT MOUSSE

 **SERVES**
**6**

 **PREP TIME**
**130**
MINUTES

 **COOK TIME**
**/**
MINUTES

**1.** Soak the gelatin in 1/2 cup coconut milk. Meanwhile, whip the egg whites to form soft peaks

**2.** Warm the gelatin mixture. Stir until gelatin melts.

**3.** Blend all ingredients except egg white until well incorporated. Gently fold in the egg whites.

**4.** Add liquid stevia to taste

**5.** Divide the mixture into 6 3-ounce mousse cups. Refrigerate for 2 hours

- **1 cup** unsweetened coconut milk

- **2** egg whites

- **2 servings** vanilla protein powder

- **1/2 teaspoon** coconut extract

- **1 teaspoon** unflavored gelatin powder

- liquid stevia to taste

| CALORIES | CARBS | SUGAR | FAT | PROTEIN | SODIUM |
|----------|-------|-------|-----|---------|--------|
| 65 | 2.6 | 0.7 | 1.5 | 10.2 | 76 |
| KCAL | GRAMS | GRAMS | GRAMS | GRAMS | MILLIGRAMS |

# SKINNY EGGNOG MOUSSE

 **SERVES**
**6**

 **PREP TIME**
**130**
MINUTES

 **COOK TIME**
**/**
MINUTES

- **1 1/2 cups** skim milk

- **2** egg whites

- **1** egg yolk

- **1 1/2 servings** vanilla protein powder

- **1/2 teaspoon** vanilla extract

- **1 teaspoon** unflavored gelatin powder

- liquid stevia to taste

**1.** Soak the gelatin in 1/2 cup of milk. Meanwhile, combine the eggs and vanilla extract.

**2.** Warm the gelatin mixture. Stir until gelatin melts.

**3.** Combine all ingredients. Add stevia to taste.

**4.** Divide the mixture into 6 3-ounce mousse cups. Refrigerate for 2 hours

| CALORIES | CARBS | SUGAR | FAT | PROTEIN | SODIUM |
|----------|-------|-------|-----|---------|--------|
| 75 | 4.7 | 3.4 | 1.3 | 10.5 | 86 |
| KCAL | GRAMS | GRAMS | GRAMS | GRAMS | MILLIGRAMS |

# CHINESE ALMOND CURD

 **SERVES** 4

 **PREP TIME** 130 MINUTES

 **COOK TIME** / MINUTES

**1.** Soak the gelatin in 1/4 cup of the skim milk. Warm the mixture and dissolve the gelatin.

**2.** Blend all ingredients until well incorporate.

**3.** Add liquid stevia to taste

**4.** Divide the mixture into 4 3-ounce mousse cups. Refrigerate for 2 hours.

- **1 cup** skim milk

- **1/4 cup** unsweetened condensed milk

- **3/4 serving** vanilla protein powder

- **1/2 teaspoon** almond extract

- **1 teaspoon** unflavored gelatin powder

- liquid stevia to taste

| CALORIES | CARBS | SUGAR | FAT | PROTEIN | SODIUM |
|---|---|---|---|---|---|
| 80 | 6.0 | 4.8 | 1.5 | 10.0 | 67 |
| KCAL | GRAMS | GRAMS | GRAMS | GRAMS | MILLIGRAMS |

# BLACK TEA AND MILK MOUSSE

 **SERVES**
**6**

 **PREP TIME**
**140**
MINUTES

 **COOK TIME**
**/**
MINUTES

- **1 cup** skim milk

- **1/2 cup** fat-free half-and-half, whipped

- **2 servings** vanilla protein powder

- **1** decaf black tea bag

- **1 teaspoon** unflavored gelatin powder

- liquid stevia to taste

**1.** Soak the gelatin in the water for 10 minutes. Warm the mixture until gelatin dissolve

**2.** Simmer 1/4 cup milk with the tea bag for 10 minutes.

**3.** Blend all ingredients except cream until well incorporated. Gently fold in the whipped cream.

**4.** Add liquid stevia to taste

**5.** Divide the mixture into 6 3-ounce mousse cups. Refrigerate for 2 hours

| CALORIES | CARBS | SUGAR | FAT | PROTEIN | SODIUM |
|---|---|---|---|---|---|
| 76 | 5.9 | 3.5 | 0.9 | 10.8 | 89 |
| KCAL | GRAMS | GRAMS | GRAMS | GRAMS | MILLIGRAMS |

# VANILLA CINNAMON MOUSSE

 **SERVES** **6**

 **PREP TIME** **4** HOURS

 **COOK TIME** **/** MINUTES

**1.** Soak the cinnamon stick in the milk for 2 hours. Carefully remove all solid.

**2.** Soak the gelatin in the water for 10 minutes.

**3.** Blend all ingredients except cream until well incorporated. Gently fold in the whipped cream.

**4.** Add liquid stevia to taste

**5.** Divide the mixture into 6 3-ounce mousse cups. Refrigerate for 2 hours

- **1 cup** skim milk

- **1 tablespoon** water

- **1/4 cup** fat-free half-and-half, whipped

- **1 stick** cinnamon

- **1 1/2 servings** vanilla protein powder

- **1 teaspoon** unflavored gelatin powder

- **1/2 teaspoon** vanilla extract

- liquid stevia to taste

| CALORIES | CARBS | SUGAR | FAT | PROTEIN | SODIUM |
|----------|-------|-------|-----|---------|--------|
| 71 | 5.1 | 3.0 | 0.8 | 10.6 | 79 |
| KCAL | GRAMS | GRAMS | GRAMS | GRAMS | MILLIGRAMS |

# KELP AND TOFU MISO SOUP

**SERVES**
**4**

**PREP TIME**
**5**
MINUTES

**COOK TIME**
**20**
MINUTES

- **1 piece** dried Kelp, cut into strips

- **1/2 block** silken tofu, cubed

- **1 1/2 tablespoons** miso paste

- **2 cups** water

1. In a medium pot, Add water and peas. Simmer for 5 minutes.

2. Stir in miso paste. Add Tofu. Simmer for another 5 minutes

3. Blend the soup until smooth. Thin with water if necessary.

4. Pass the soup through a strainer to remove large chunks.

| CALORIES | CARBS | SUGAR | FAT | PROTEIN | SODIUM |
|----------|-------|-------|-----|---------|--------|
| 39 | 2.4 | 1.1 | 1.6 | 4.1 | 199 |
| KCAL | GRAMS | GRAMS | GRAMS | GRAMS | MILLIGRAMS |

# SHRIMP AND GREEN PEA SOUP

 **SERVES** 8

 **PREP TIME** 5 MINUTES

 **COOK TIME** 20 MINUTES

**1.** In a medium pot, Add broth and kelp. Bring to a boil and simmer for 5 minutes.

**2.** Add shrimp and milk. Simmer for another 5 minutes. Season with salt.

**3.** Blend the soup until smooth. Thin with water if necessary.

**4.** Pass the soup through a strainer to remove large chunks.

- **12 ounces** frozen shrimps, thawed

- **1** 8.5-ounce **can** green peas, rinsed and drained

- **3 cups** fat-free low sodium chicken broth

- **1 cup** skim milk

- **1/4 teaspoon** salt

| CALORIES | CARBS | SUGAR | FAT | PROTEIN | SODIUM |
|----------|-------|-------|-----|---------|--------|
| 58 | 4.5 | 2.4 | 0.4 | 10.4 | 293 |
| KCAL | GRAMS | GRAMS | GRAMS | GRAMS | MILLIGRAMS |

# CREAM OF SEAFOOD SOUP

 **SERVES** 16

 **PREP TIME** 5 MINUTES

 **COOK TIME** 25 MINUTES

- **1/2 pound** white fish fillets, cubed

- **1/2 pound** frozen shrimps, thawed and chopped

- **2** 4-ounce **cans** crab meat, drained

- **1** medium onion, peeled and chopped

- **4 cups** skim milk

- **2 cups** fat-free low sodium chicken broth

- **2 cups** fat-free half and half

- **1 teaspoon** salt

- Nonstick cooking spray

1. In a large pot, sauté the onion until fragrant.

2. Add all ingredients and simmer for 10 minutes. Season with salt

3. Blend the soup until smooth. Thin with water if necessary.

4. Pass the soup through a strainer to remove large chunks.

| CALORIES | CARBS | SUGAR | FAT | PROTEIN | SODIUM |
|---|---|---|---|---|---|
| 74 | 6.6 | 4.3 | 0.9 | 11.2 | 341 |
| KCAL | GRAMS | GRAMS | GRAMS | GRAMS | MILLIGRAMS |

# CHEESY PUMPKIN SOUP

 SERVES
**8**

 PREP TIME
**5**
MINUTES

 COOK TIME
**25**
MINUTES

**1.** In a large pot, sauté the onion until fragrant.

**2.** Add all ingredients except cheese and simmer for 10 minutes

**3.** Remove from heat and stir in cheese in batches

**4.** Blend the soup until smooth. Thin with water if necessary.

**5.** Pass the soup through a strainer to remove large chunks.

- **1 cup** canned pumpkin

- **1/2** medium onion, peeled and chopped

- **2 cloves** garlic, minced

- **1 cup** shredded low-fat cheddar cheese

- **1 cup** skim milk

- **1 cup** fat-free low sodium chicken broth

- **1/2 teaspoon** salt

- Nonstick cooking spray

| CALORIES | CARBS | SUGAR | FAT | PROTEIN | SODIUM |
|----------|-------|-------|-----|---------|--------|
| **51** | **5.2** | **2.5** | **1.1** | **5.1** | **291** |
| KCAL | GRAMS | GRAMS | GRAMS | GRAMS | MILLIGRAMS |

# MEXICAN CHICKEN SOUP

 **SERVES**
2

 **PREP TIME**
5
MINUTES

 **COOK TIME**
/
MINUTES

- **1** 12-ounce **can** chicken breast

- **1** 10-ounce **can** diced tomatoes with chilies

- **1 cup** canned black beans

- **1/4 cup** low-fat shredded Mexican cheese

- **3 cups** fat-free low sodium chicken broth

- **1 cup** fat-free sour cream

- **2 tablespoons** chopped fresh cilantro

- **1/2 teaspoon** garlic powder

- **1/2 teaspoon** salt

**1.** In a large broth, add broth and tomatoes. Bring it to a boil. Then add chicken and beans. Simmer for 20 minutes.

**2.** Remove from heat, stir in sour cream, cheese and cilantro. Season with salt and garlic powder

**3.** Blend the soup until smooth. Thin with water if necessary.

**4.** Pass the soup through a strainer to remove large chunks.

| CALORIES | CARBS | SUGAR | FAT | PROTEIN | SODIUM |
|----------|-------|-------|-----|---------|--------|
| 73 | 7.8 | 1.8 | 1.0 | 7.6 | 358 |
| KCAL | GRAMS | GRAMS | GRAMS | GRAMS | MILLIGRAMS |

# CREAMY PESTO CHICKEN SOUP

 **SERVES** 2

 **PREP TIME** 5 MINUTES

 **COOK TIME** / MINUTES

1. In a large pot, sauté the onion until fragrant.

2. Add broth, chicken and pesto. Bring it to a boil. Simmer for 20 minutes. Add milk and bring it to a simmer

3. Remove from heat, stir in sour cream and cheese. Season with salt.

4. Blend the soup until smooth. Thin with water if necessary.

5. Pass the soup through a strainer to remove large chunks.

- **1** 12-ounce **can** chicken breast

- **1/2** medium onion, peeled and chopped

- **1 cup** low-fat shredded cheddar cheese

- **2 cups** fat-free chicken broth

- **1 cup** skim milk

- **1/2 cup** fat-free sour cream

- **3 tablespoons** low-fat pesto

- **1/2 teaspoon** salt

- Nonstick cooking spray

| CALORIES | CARBS | SUGAR | FAT | PROTEIN | SODIUM |
|---|---|---|---|---|---|
| 64 | 3.8 | 1.7 | 1.6 | 8.3 | 347 |
| KCAL | GRAMS | GRAMS | GRAMS | GRAMS | MILLIGRAMS |

# BUFFALO CHICKEN SOUP

- **1** 12-ounce **can** chicken breast

- **1/2** medium onion, peeled and chopped

- **1 cup** low-fat shredded cheddar cheese

- **2 1/2 cups** fat-free chicken broth

- **1 cup** fat-free half-and-half

- **1/4 cup** buffalo sauce

- **1/2 teaspoon** salt

- Nonstick cooking spray

**1.** In a large pot, sauté the onion until fragrant.

**2.** Add broth, chicken and buffalo sauce. Bring it to a boil. Simmer for 20 minutes. Add milk and bring it to a simmer

**3.** Remove from heat, stir in half-and-half and cheese. Season with salt.

**4.** Blend the soup until smooth. Thin with water if necessary.

**5.** Pass the soup through a strainer to remove large chunks.

| CALORIES | CARBS | SUGAR | FAT | PROTEIN | SODIUM |
|---|---|---|---|---|---|
| 57 | 3.1 | 1.1 | 1.5 | 7.8 | 479 |
| KCAL | GRAMS | GRAMS | GRAMS | GRAMS | MILLIGRAMS |

# CREAMY CRAB BISQUE

 **SERVES**
**12**

 **PREP TIME**
**5**
MINUTES

 **COOK TIME**
**40**
MINUTES

1. In a large pot, sauté the onion and bell peppers until fragrant.

2. Add broth, crab, herbs and spice. Bring it to a boil. Simmer for 20 minutes. Add milk and bring it to a simmer

3. Remove from heat, stir in sour cream. Season with salt.

4. Blend the soup until smooth. Thin with water if necessary.

5. Pass the soup through a strainer to remove large chunks.

- **3** 6-ounce **cans** crab meat

- **1/2** medium onion, peeled and chopped

- **1** medium bell pepper, chopped

- **2 cups** fat-free low sodium chicken broth

- **1 1/2 cups** skim milk

- **1/4 cup** fat-free sour cream

- **2** bay leaves

- **1 teaspoon** smoke paprika

- **1 teaspoon** thyme

- **1/2 teaspoon** salt

| CALORIES | CARBS | SUGAR | FAT | PROTEIN | SODIUM |
|----------|-------|-------|-----|---------|--------|
| 54 | 3.9 | 2.2 | 0.8 | 7.7 | 351 |
| KCAL | GRAMS | GRAMS | GRAMS | GRAMS | MILLIGRAMS |

# CLAM CHOWDER

SERVES
**12**

PREP TIME
**5**
MINUTES

COOK TIME
**40**
MINUTES

- 2 10-ounce **cans** whole baby clams
- **1/2** medium onion, peeled and chopped
- **1 cup** fat-free low sodium chicken broth
- **1 cup** clam juice
- **1 cup** skim milk
- **1 cup** fat-free half and half
- **2** bay leaves
- **1 tablespoon** chopped fresh parsley
- **1 tablespoon** chopped fresh chives
- **1 teaspoon** chopped fresh thyme
- **1/2 teaspoon** salt
- Nonstick cooking spray

1. In a large pot, sauté the onion until fragrant.

2. Add broth, clam juice, baby clams and herbs. Bring it to a boil. Simmer for 20 minutes. Add milk and bring it to a simmer

3. Remove from heat, stir in cream. Season with salt.

4. Blend the soup until smooth. Thin with water if necessary.

5. Pass the soup through a strainer to remove large chunks.

| CALORIES | CARBS | SUGAR | FAT | PROTEIN | SODIUM |
|---|---|---|---|---|---|
| 54 | 5.3 | 2.1 | 1.1 | 9.4 | 433 |
| KCAL | GRAMS | GRAMS | GRAMS | GRAMS | MILLIGRAMS |

# PORTOBELLO CHEDDAR SOUP

 **SERVES**
**12**

 **PREP TIME**
**10**
MINUTES

 **COOK TIME**
**35**
MINUTES

**1.** In a large pot, sauté the onion, mushroom and garlic until fragrant.

**2.** Add broth and herbs. Bring it to a boil. Simmer for 20 minutes. Add milk and bring it to a simmer.

**3.** Remove from heat, stir in cream and cheese. Season with salt.

**4.** Blend the soup until smooth. Thin with water if necessary.

**5.** Pass the soup through a strainer to remove large chunks.

- **20 ounces** Portobello mushroom, sliced
- **1/2** medium onion, peeled and chopped
- **3 cloves** garlic
- **2 cups** fat-free low-sodium chicken broth
- **1 cup** low-fat shredded cheddar cheese
- **1 cup** skim milk
- **1/2 cup** fat-free half and half
- **1** bay leave
- **2 tablespoons** chopped fresh parsley
- **1/2 teaspoon** salt
- Nonstick cooking spray

| CALORIES | CARBS | SUGAR | FAT | PROTEIN | SODIUM |
|---|---|---|---|---|---|
| 46 | 4.5 | 1.5 | 0.8 | 5.3 | 218 |
| KCAL | GRAMS | GRAMS | GRAMS | GRAMS | MILLIGRAMS |

# CHEESEBURGER SOUP

**SERVES**
**12**

**PREP TIME**
**10**
MINUTES

**COOK TIME**
**35**
MINUTES

- **1 pound** 97/3 lean ground beef

- **1 medium** onion, peeled and chopped

- **2 cloves** garlic, minced

- **3 cups** fat-free low sodium chicken broth, divided

- **1 cup** low-fat evaporated milk

- **1 cup** low-fat shredded cheddar cheese

- **1/2 teaspoon** paprika

- **1/2 teaspoon** salt

- **1/4 teaspoon** ground black pepper

- Nonstick Cooking Spray

1. In a large pot, sauté the onion, mushroom and garlic until fragrant. Set aside.

2. Brown the beef. Then add all ingredients except cheese and seasoning. Simmer for 20 minutes.

3. Remove from heat, stir in cheese . Season with salt, pepper and paprika.

4. Blend the soup until smooth. Thin with water if necessary.

5. Pass the soup through a strainer to remove large chunks.

| CALORIES | CARBS | SUGAR | FAT | PROTEIN | SODIUM |
|---|---|---|---|---|---|
| 82 | 3.2 | 1.4 | 2.4 | 12.2 | 233 |
| KCAL | GRAMS | GRAMS | GRAMS | GRAMS | MILLIGRAMS |

# CAULIFLOWER BISQUE

 **SERVES** **12**

 **PREP TIME** **10** MINUTES

 **COOK TIME** **35** MINUTES

1. In a large pot, sauté the onion and garlic until fragrant. Set aside.

2. Sauté the bacon until crispy. Then add all ingredients except cheese and seasoning. Simmer for 20 minutes.

3. Remove from heat. Stir in cheese . Season with salt and pepper.

4. Blend the soup until smooth. Thin with water if necessary.

5. Pass the soup through a strainer to remove large chunks.

- **1 pound** cauliflower, chopped
- **6 slices** extra lean turkey bacon, chopped
- **1** medium onion, peeled and chopped
- **2 cloves** garlic, minced
- **1 cup** low-fat shredded cheddar cheese
- **2 cups** fat-free low sodium chicken broth
- **1 cup** skim milk
- **1 cup** fat-free half-and-half
- **1** bay leave
- **2 tablespoons** chopped fresh parsley
- **1/2 teaspoon** salt
- **1/4 teaspoon** ground black pepper
- Nonstick Cooking Spray

| CALORIES | CARBS | SUGAR | FAT | PROTEIN | SODIUM |
|---|---|---|---|---|---|
| 62 | 6.5 | 2.9 | 2.2 | 5.7 | 296 |
| KCAL | GRAMS | GRAMS | GRAMS | GRAMS | MILLIGRAMS |

# TOMATO AND BEEF SOUP

 **SERVES**
**12**

 **PREP TIME**
**10**
MINUTES

 **COOK TIME**
**35**
MINUTES

- **1 pound** 97/3 lean ground beef
- **1 cup** chopped tomatoes
- **1 medium** onion, peeled and chopped
- **1 bell peppers**, chopped
- **1 medium** carrot, peeled and chopped
- **2 cloves** garlic, minced
- **3 cups** fat-free low sodium chicken broth
- **2 tablespoons** tomato paste
- **2 tablespoons** chopped fresh parsley
- **1/2 teaspoon** oregano
- **1/2 teaspoon** salt
- **1/4 teaspoon** pepper
- Nonstick Cooking Spray

1. In a large pot, sauté the onion, bell peppers and carrot until fragrant. Set aside.

2. Brown the beef. Then add all ingredients except seasoning. Simmer for 20 minutes. Season with salt and pepper.

3. Blend the soup until smooth. Thin with water if necessary.

4. Pass the soup through a strainer to remove large chunks.

| CALORIES | CARBS | SUGAR | FAT | PROTEIN | SODIUM |
|----------|-------|-------|-----|---------|--------|
| 64 | 4.5 | 1.7 | 1.4 | 9.2 | 137 |
| KCAL | GRAMS | GRAMS | GRAMS | GRAMS | MILLIGRAMS |

# CHEESY BROCCOLI SOUP

 **SERVES** 12

 **PREP TIME** 10 MINUTES

 **COOK TIME** 35 MINUTES

1. In a large pot, sauté the onion and garlic until fragrant. Set aside.

2. Add all ingredients except cheese and seasoning. Simmer for 30 minutes.

3. Remove from heat. Stir in cheese. Season with salt and pepper.

4. Blend the soup until smooth. Thin with water if necessary.

5. Pass the soup through a strainer to remove large chunks.

- **1 pound** broccoli, chopped

- **1** medium onion, chopped

- **2 cloves** garlic, minced

- **1 1/2 cups** low-fat shredded cheddar cheese

- **2 cups** skim milk

- **2 cups** fat-free low sodium chicken broth

- **1/2 teaspoon** salt

- **1/4 teaspoon** ground black pepper

- Nonstick cooking spray

| CALORIES | CARBS | SUGAR | FAT | PROTEIN | SODIUM |
|---|---|---|---|---|---|
| 58 | 6.1 | 2.5 | 1.1 | 6.3 | 262 |
| KCAL | GRAMS | GRAMS | GRAMS | GRAMS | MILLIGRAMS |

# ITALIAN SHRIMP SOUP

**SERVES**
**12**

**PREP TIME**
**10**
MINUTES

**COOK TIME**
**50**
MINUTES

- **1 pound** frozen shrimps, thawed and chopped

- **3 cups** fat-free low sodium chicken broth

- **1 cup** chopped tomatoes

- **1 cup** clam juice

- **4 cloves** garlic, minced

- **2 tablespoons** tomato paste

- **1 tablespoon** rosemary

- **1 tablespoon** Italian seasoning

- **1 teaspoon** celery seed

- **1 teaspoon** fennel seed

- **1/2 teaspoon** salt

- **1/4 teaspoon** pepper

- Nonstick cooking spray

1. Put rosemary, Italian seasoning, celery seed and fennel seed in a mesh tea bag.

2. In a large pot, sauté garlic until fragrant.

3. Add broth, tomatoes, clam juice, tomato paste and the prepared spice bag. Simmer for 30 minutes

4. Add shrimp and cook for another 10 minutes. Remove the spice bag.

5. Blend the soup until smooth. Thin with water if necessary.

6. Pass the soup through a strainer to remove large chunks.

| CALORIES | CARBS | SUGAR | FAT | PROTEIN | SODIUM |
|---|---|---|---|---|---|
| 42 | 1.9 | 1.1 | 0.3 | 8.3 | 306 |
| KCAL | GRAMS | GRAMS | GRAMS | GRAMS | MILLIGRAMS |

# ROASTED BEET AND FETA SOUP

**SERVES**
**12**

**PREP TIME**
**10**
MINUTES

**COOK TIME**
**80**
MINUTES

1. Preheat the oven to 400°F

2. In a large bowl, toss beetroot with thyme, salt and pepper. Spread the beetroot on a baking sheet and spray with cooking spray. Bake for 30 minutes or until tender

3. In a large pot, sauté the onion, leek and garlic until fragrant.

4. Add all ingredients except cream, cheese and milk. Bring it to a boil. Simmer for 30 minutes. Add milk and bring it to a simmer.

5. Remove from heat, stir in cream and cheese. Season with salt.

6. Blend the soup until smooth. Thin with water if necessary.

7. Pass the soup through a strainer to remove large chunks.

- 3 medium beetroot, peeled and cubed
- 1 stalk leek, chopped
- 1/2 medium onion, peeled and chopped
- 2 cloves garlic, minced
- 2 cups skim milk
- 1 cup fat-free low sodium chicken broth
- 1 cup fat-free feta cheese
- 1/2 cup fat-free half-and half
- 2 tablespoons chopped fresh parsley
- 1 tablespoon chopped fresh thyme
- 1/2 teaspoon salt
- 1/4 teaspoon ground black pepper
- Non-stick cooking spray

| CALORIES | CARBS | SUGAR | FAT | PROTEIN | SODIUM |
|----------|-------|-------|-----|---------|--------|
| 46 | 7.0 | 4.1 | 0.2 | 4.5 | 291 |
| KCAL | GRAMS | GRAMS | GRAMS | GRAMS | MILLIGRAMS |

# ITALIAN CHICKEN PUREE

 **SERVES**
4

 **PREP TIME**
10
MINUTES

 **COOK TIME**
10
MINUTES

- **8 ounces** boneless skinless chicken breast, boiled and shredded

- **1 cup** fat-free low sodium chicken broth

- **1/4 cup** fat-free grated parmesan cheese

- **1 clove** garlic

- **1 tablespoon** chopped fresh parsley

- **1 tablespoon** oregano

- **1/2 teaspoon** garlic powder

- **1/4 teaspoon** salt

1. Blend all ingredients with half of the broth until smooth. Thin with the remaining broth until desired consistency is reached.

2. Pass the puree through a strainer to remove large chunks.

3. Reheat the puree in the microwave if desired

| CALORIES | CARBS | SUGAR | FAT | PROTEIN | SODIUM |
|---|---|---|---|---|---|
| 76 | 3.8 | 0.0 | 1.5 | 12.6 | 407 |
| KCAL | GRAMS | GRAMS | GRAMS | GRAMS | MILLIGRAMS |

# CAJUN CHICKEN PUREE

 **SERVES**
4

 **PREP TIME**
10
MINUTES

 **COOK TIME**
10
MINUTES

1. In a sauce pan, sauté the onion and garlic until fragrant.

2. Blend all ingredients with half of the broth until smooth. Thin with the remaining broth until desired consistency is reached.

3. Pass the puree through a strainer to remove large chunks.

4. Reheat the puree in the microwave if desired

- **8 ounces** boneless skinless chicken breast, boiled and shredded

- **3/4 cup** fat-free low sodium chicken broth

- **1/4 cup** chopped onion

- **1 clove** garlic

- **1 tablespoon** Cajun seasoning

- **1/4 teaspoon** salt

- Nonstick cooking spray

| CALORIES | CARBS | SUGAR | FAT | PROTEIN | SODIUM |
|---|---|---|---|---|---|
| 62 | 1.1 | 0.4 | 1.5 | 11.5 | 474 |
| KCAL | GRAMS | GRAMS | GRAMS | GRAMS | MILLIGRAMS |

# CREAMY PUMPKIN CHICKEN SOUP

 **SERVES**
**6**

 **PREP TIME**
**10**
MINUTES

 **COOK TIME**
**10**
MINUTES

- **8 ounces** boneless skinless chicken breast, boiled and shredded

- **1/2 cup** canned pumpkin puree

- **1/4 cup** low-fat shredded cheddar cheese

- **1 cup** skim milk

- **1 tablespoon** chopped fresh chives

- **1/2 teaspoon** Dijon mustard

- **1/4 teaspoon** salt

**1.** Blend all ingredients with half of the broth until smooth. Thin with the remaining broth until desired consistency is reached.

**2.** Pass the puree through a strainer to remove large chunks.

**3.** Reheat the puree in the microwave if desired

| CALORIES | CARBS | SUGAR | FAT | PROTEIN | SODIUM |
|----------|-------|-------|-----|---------|--------|
| 68 | 3.6 | 2.5 | 1.4 | 10.1 | 292 |
| KCAL | GRAMS | GRAMS | GRAMS | GRAMS | MILLIGRAMS |

# THAI PEANUT CHICKEN PUREE

 SERVES
**4**

 PREP TIME
**10**
MINUTES

 COOK TIME
**10**
MINUTES

**1.** Blend all ingredients with half of the broth until smooth. Thin with the remaining broth until desired consistency is reached.

**2.** Pass the puree through a strainer to remove large chunks.

**3.** Reheat the puree in the microwave if desired

- **8 ounces** boneless skinless chicken breast, boiled and shredded

- **1 cup** fat-free low sodium chicken broth

- **1/4 cup** powdered peanut butter

- **1 clove** garlic

- **1 tablespoon** chopped green onion

- **1 tablespoon** low sodium soy sauce

- **2 teaspoons** grated fresh ginger root

- **1/2 teaspoon** vinegar

- Salt and pepper to taste

| CALORIES | CARBS | SUGAR | FAT | PROTEIN | SODIUM |
|---|---|---|---|---|---|
| 86 | 3.9 | 1.6 | 2.3 | 13.8 | 313 |
| KCAL | GRAMS | GRAMS | GRAMS | GRAMS | MILLIGRAMS |

# TERIYAKI CHICKEN PUREE

 **SERVES** **4**

 **PREP TIME** **10** MINUTES

 **COOK TIME** **10** MINUTES

- **8 ounces** boneless skinless chicken breast, boiled and shredded

- **1 cup** fat-free low sodium chicken broth

- **1 clove** garlic

- **2 tablespoons** low-sodium soy sauce

- **1 tablespoon** Truvia, preferably brown sugar blend

- **1 tablespoon** grated fresh ginger root

**1.** Blend all ingredients with half of the broth until smooth. Thin with the remaining broth until desired consistency is reached.

**2.** Pass the puree through a strainer to remove large chunks.

**3.** Reheat the puree in the microwave if desired

| CALORIES | CARBS | SUGAR | FAT | PROTEIN | SODIUM |
|----------|-------|-------|-----|---------|--------|
| 72 | 4.0 | 1.5 | 1.5 | 12.0 | 421 |
| KCAL | GRAMS | GRAMS | GRAMS | GRAMS | MILLIGRAMS |

# LEMON MUSTARD CHICKEN PUREE

 SERVES
4

 PREP TIME
10
MINUTES

 COOK TIME
10
MINUTES

1. Blend all ingredients with half of the broth until smooth. Thin with the remaining broth until desired consistency is reached.

2. Pass the puree through a strainer to remove large chunks.

3. Reheat the puree in the microwave if desired

- **8 ounces** boneless skinless chicken breast, boiled and shredded

- **3/4 cup** fat-free low sodium chicken broth

- **2 tablespoons** lemon juice

- **2 tablespoons** Dijon mustard

- **1 teaspoon** Truvia, preferably brown sugar blend

- **1/4 teaspoon** salt

| CALORIES | CARBS | SUGAR | FAT | PROTEIN | SODIUM |
|---|---|---|---|---|---|
| 69 | 1.7 | 0.7 | 1.5 | 11.4 | 451 |
| KCAL | GRAMS | GRAMS | GRAMS | GRAMS | MILLIGRAMS |

# CREAMY WORCESTERSHIRE CHICKEN PUREE

 **SERVES**
4

 **PREP TIME**
10
MINUTES

 **COOK TIME**
10
MINUTES

- **8 ounces** boneless skinless chicken breast, boiled and shredded

- **1/2 cup** skim milk

- **1/2 cup** fat-free half-and-half

- **1 tablespoon** Worcestershire sauce

- **1/4 teaspoon** salt

1. Blend all ingredients with half of the broth until smooth. Thin with the remaining broth until desired consistency is reached.

2. Pass the puree through a strainer to remove large chunks.

3. Reheat the puree in the microwave if desired

| CALORIES | CARBS | SUGAR | FAT | PROTEIN | SODIUM |
|----------|-------|-------|-----|---------|--------|
| 86 | 4.9 | 3.3 | 1.9 | 12.8 | 343 |
| KCAL | GRAMS | GRAMS | GRAMS | GRAMS | MILLIGRAMS |

# INDIAN BUTTER CHICKEN PUREE

 **SERVES** 12

 **PREP TIME** 10 MINUTES

 **COOK TIME** 10 MINUTES

**1.** Blend all ingredients with half of the broth until smooth. Thin with the remaining broth until desired consistency is reached.

**2.** Pass the puree through a strainer to remove large chunks.

**3.** Reheat the puree in the microwave if desired

- **8 ounces** boneless skinless chicken breast, boiled and shredded

- **1/2 cup** skim milk

- **1/2 cup** chopped tomatoes

- **2 tablespoons** fat-free Greek Yogurt

- **1 clove** garlic

- **1/2 tablespoon** curry powder

- **1/2 teaspoon** salt

| CALORIES | CARBS | SUGAR | FAT | PROTEIN | SODIUM |
|---|---|---|---|---|---|
| 75 | 2.9 | 2.2 | 1.6 | 12.8 | 419 |
| KCAL | GRAMS | GRAMS | GRAMS | GRAMS | MILLIGRAMS |

# PARMESAN PESTO TILAPIA

SERVES
**4**

PREP TIME
**10**
MINUTES

COOK TIME
**10**
MINUTES

- **8 ounces** tilapia fillet, steamed and chopped

- **3/4 cup** fat-free low sodium chicken broth

- **1/4 cup** chopped tomatoes

- **2 tablespoons** fat-free parmesan cheese

- **1 tablespoon** low-fat pesto

- **1 teaspoon** lemon juice

- dash of salt and pepper

**1.** Blend all ingredients with half of the broth until smooth. Thin with the remaining broth until desired consistency is reached.

**2.** Pass the puree through a strainer to remove large chunks.

**3.** Reheat the puree in the microwave if desired

| CALORIES | CARBS | SUGAR | FAT | PROTEIN | SODIUM |
|----------|-------|-------|-----|---------|--------|
| 66 | 0.6 | 0.3 | 1.9 | 10.9 | 189 |
| KCAL | GRAMS | GRAMS | GRAMS | GRAMS | MILLIGRAMS |

# SALMON RILLETTES

 SERVES
**3**

 PREP TIME
**10**
MINUTES

 COOK TIME
**10**
MINUTES

**1.** Blend all ingredients until smooth. Thin with water until desired consistency is reached.

**2.** Pass the puree through a strainer to remove large chunks.

- **1** 6-ounce **can** pink salmon, drained

- **2 tablespoons** chopped shallot

- **2 tablespoons** fat-free Greek yogurt

- **1/2 tablespoon** chopped fresh chives

- **1/2 teaspoon** lemon juice

- dash of salt

| CALORIES | CARBS | SUGAR | FAT | PROTEIN | SODIUM |
|---|---|---|---|---|---|
| **68** | **1.4** | **0.7** | **1.0** | **13.8** | **319** |
| KCAL | GRAMS | GRAMS | GRAMS | GRAMS | MILLIGRAMS |

# MARYLAND CRAB PUREE

 **SERVES**
3

 **PREP TIME**
**10**
MINUTES

 **COOK TIME**
**10**
MINUTES

- **1** 6-ounce **can** crab meat, drained

- **2 tablespoons** chopped shallot

- **2 tablespoons** low fat mayonnaise

- **1/2 teaspoon** Old Bay seasoning

1. Blend all ingredients until smooth. Thin with water until desired consistency is reached.

2. Pass the puree through a strainer to remove large chunks.

| CALORIES | CARBS | SUGAR | FAT | PROTEIN | SODIUM |
|---|---|---|---|---|---|
| 55 | 2.5 | 1.2 | 1.7 | 8.2 | 494 |
| KCAL | GRAMS | GRAMS | GRAMS | GRAMS | MILLIGRAMS |

# SHRIMP SCAMPI PUREE

**SERVES**
**6**

**PREP TIME**
**5**
MINUTES

**COOK TIME**
**15**
MINUTES

**1.** In a sauce pan, sauté the garlic until fragrant. Add Shrimp, lemon juice and red pepper flakes. Cook for another 2 minutes

**2.** Remove from heat. Add the remaining ingredients. Stir until incorporated.

**3.** Blend all ingredients until smooth. Thin with water until desired consistency is reached.

**4.** Pass the puree through a strainer to remove large chunks.

- **8 ounces** frozen shrimp, thawed and chopped

- **1 clove** garlic, minced

- **2 tablespoons** lemon juice

- **1/4 cup** low-fat cream cheese

- **1/4 cup** fat-free sour cream

- **1/4 cup** fat-free parmesan

- **2 tablespoons** low-fat mayonnaise

- **1/4 teaspoon** red pepper flakes

| CALORIES | CARBS | SUGAR | FAT | PROTEIN | SODIUM |
|----------|-------|-------|-----|---------|--------|
| 88 | 3.5 | 1.7 | 2.6 | 11.2 | 382 |
| KCAL | GRAMS | GRAMS | GRAMS | GRAMS | MILLIGRAMS |

# PINTO BEAN MASH

 **SERVES**
**6**

 **PREP TIME**
**10**
MINUTES

 **COOK TIME**
**10**
MINUTES

- **1** 15-ounce **can** pinto bean, rinsed and drained

- **3 slices** canned jalapeno pepper, seeded

- **1 tablespoon** white vinegar

- **1/4 teaspoon** Truvia

- **1/4 teaspoon** paprika

- **1/4 teaspoon** onion powder

- **1/4 teaspoon** salt

**1.** Blend all ingredients until smooth. Thin with water until desired consistency is reached.

**2.** Pass the puree through a strainer to remove large chunks.

| CALORIES | CARBS | SUGAR | FAT | PROTEIN | SODIUM |
|---|---|---|---|---|---|
| 71 | 12.8 | 0.5 | 0.7 | 3.7 | 431 |
| KCAL | GRAMS | GRAMS | GRAMS | GRAMS | MILLIGRAMS |

# HUMMUS FETA PUREE

 SERVES
3

 PREP TIME
**10**
MINUTES

 COOK TIME
**10**
MINUTES

**1.** Blend all ingredients until smooth. Thin with water until desired consistency is reached.

**2.** Pass the puree through a strainer to remove large chunks.

- 1/4 cup Hummus

- 2 ounces fat-free Feta Cheese

- 2 teaspoons roasted red pepper

| CALORIES | CARBS | SUGAR | FAT | PROTEIN | SODIUM |
|----------|-------|-------|-----|---------|--------|
| 77 | 4.7 | 1.3 | 3.7 | 6.0 | 263 |
| KCAL | GRAMS | GRAMS | GRAMS | GRAMS | MILLIGRAMS |

# CURRY TOFU PUREE

 **SERVES**
4

 **PREP TIME**
10
MINUTES

 **COOK TIME**
10
MINUTES

- **1** 12-ounce **block** silken tofu, Cubed and steamed

- **1/2 teaspoon** salt

- **1/2 teaspoon** garlic powder

- **1/2 teaspoon** ground cumin

- **1/4 teaspoon** chili powder

- **1/4 teaspoon** turmeric

**1.** Blend all ingredients until smooth. Thin with water until desired consistency is reached.

**2.** Reheat the puree in the microwave if desired

| CALORIES | CARBS | SUGAR | FAT | PROTEIN | SODIUM |
|---|---|---|---|---|---|
| 71 | 3.5 | 0.0 | 3.1 | 9.1 | 289 |
| KCAL | GRAMS | GRAMS | GRAMS | GRAMS | MILLIGRAMS |

# CHEESY GARLIC CAULIFLOWER MASH

 SERVES
6

 PREP TIME
10
MINUTES

 COOK TIME
20
MINUTES

**1.** Blend all ingredients until smooth. Thin with water if necessary.

**2.** Pass the puree through a strainer to remove large chunks.

- **1** medium head cauliflower, finely chopped

- **2 cloves** garlic

- **1 cup** low-fat shredded cheddar cheese

- **1/4 cup** fat-free sour cream

- **1/2 teaspoon** salt

- **1/4 teaspoon** ground black pepper

| CALORIES | CARBS | SUGAR | FAT | PROTEIN | SODIUM |
|----------|-------|-------|-----|---------|--------|
| 68 | 7.1 | 3.1 | 1.4 | 6.8 | 391 |
| KCAL | GRAMS | GRAMS | GRAMS | GRAMS | MILLIGRAMS |

# BEEF AND VEGETABLE PUREE

**SERVES**
**4**

**PREP TIME**
**10**
MINUTES

**COOK TIME**
**20**
MINUTES

- **8 ounces** 97/3 lean ground beef

- **3/4 cup** fat-free low sodium chicken broth

- **1/4 cup** chopped onion

- **1/4 cup** chopped carrot

- **1 clove** garlic, minced

- **1 tablespoon** chopped fresh thyme

- **1/4 teaspoon** salt

- Nonstick Cooking Spray

1. In a sauce pan, sauté the garlic, onion and carrot until fragrant

2. Brown the meat. Break down into small chunks. Add herb, half of the broth and vegtables. Cover and simmer for 20 minutes

3. Blend all ingredients until smooth. Thin with the remaining broth to desired consistency.

4. Pass the puree through a strainer to remove large chunks.

| CALORIES | CARBS | SUGAR | FAT | PROTEIN | SODIUM |
|----------|-------|-------|-----|---------|--------|
| **96** | **2.0** | **0.8** | **4.0** | **11.6** | **328** |
| KCAL | GRAMS | GRAMS | GRAMS | GRAMS | MILLIGRAMS |

# BEEF CASSEROLE PUREE

 **SERVES**
**4**

 **PREP TIME**
**10**
MINUTES

 **COOK TIME**
**20**
MINUTES

**1.** Blanch the cauliflower in boiling water until soft, about 10-15 minutes. Drain and set aside

**2.** Brown the meat. Break down into small chunks. Add herb, half of the broth and vegetables. Cover and simmer for 20 minutes

**3.** Blend all ingredients until smooth. Thin with water if necessary.

**4.** Pass the puree through a strainer to remove large chunks.

- **8 ounces** 97/3 lean ground beef

- **3/4 cup** fat-free low sodium chicken broth

- **1/2 cup** chopped cauliflower

- **1 clove** garlic, minced

- **1 tablespoon** chopped fresh thyme

- **1 tablespoon** chopped fresh parsley

- **1/4 teaspoon** salt

- Nonstick Cooking Spray

| CALORIES | CARBS | SUGAR | FAT | PROTEIN | SODIUM |
|---|---|---|---|---|---|
| 126 | 6.9 | 1.1 | 4.8 | 14.4 | 378 |
| KCAL | GRAMS | GRAMS | GRAMS | GRAMS | MILLIGRAMS |

# BEEF STEW PUREE

 **SERVES**
**6**

 **PREP TIME**
**10**
MINUTES

 **COOK TIME**
**20**
MINUTES

- **8 ounces** 97/3 lean ground beef

- **1 cup** fat-free low sodium chicken broth

- **1/4 cup** finely chopped potatoes

- **1/4 cup** canned pumpkin puree

- **1/4 cup** finely chopped carrot

- **1 clove** garlic

- **2 tablespoons** low-fat shredded cheddar cheese

- **1 tablespoon** chopped fresh parsley

- **1 teaspoon** tomato paste

- **1/4 teaspoon** salt

1. In a sauce pan, sauté the potatoes and carrot until fragrant.

2. Brown the meat. Break down into small chunks. Add herb, half of the broth and vegetables. Cover and simmer for 20 minutes. Stir in cheese.

3. Blend all ingredients until smooth. Thin with water if necessary.

4. Pass the puree through a strainer to remove large chunks.

| CALORIES | CARBS | SUGAR | FAT | PROTEIN | SODIUM |
|----------|-------|-------|-----|---------|--------|
| 106 | 8.6 | 1.3 | 3.4 | 10.6 | 278 |
| KCAL | GRAMS | GRAMS | GRAMS | GRAMS | MILLIGRAMS |

# BOLOGNESE PUREE

 **SERVES**
6

 **PREP TIME**
10
MINUTES

 **COOK TIME**
20
MINUTES

**1.** In a sauce pan, sauté the onion and carrot until fragrant.

**2.** Brown the meat. Break down into small chunks. Add herbs, tomatoes, half of broth and vegetables. Cover and simmer for 20 minutes. Stir in cheese.

**3.** Blend all ingredients until smooth. Thin with water if necessary.

**4.** Pass the puree through a strainer to remove large chunks.

- **12 ounces** 97/3 lean ground beef
- **1 cup** crushed tomatoes
- **1/2 cup** fat-free low sodium chicken broth
- **1/4 cup** chopped onion
- **1/4 cup** chopped carrot
- **2 tablespoons** fat-free parmesan cheese
- **1 clove** garlic
- **1** bay leave
- **1/2 tablespoon** chopped fresh thyme
- **1 teaspoon** dried oregano
- **1/4 teaspoon** salt
- Nonstick cooking spray

| CALORIES | CARBS | SUGAR | FAT | PROTEIN | SODIUM |
|----------|-------|-------|-----|---------|--------|
| 111 | 4.4 | 1.9 | 4.0 | 12.3 | 391 |
| KCAL | GRAMS | GRAMS | GRAMS | GRAMS | MILLIGRAMS |

# APPLE CUCUMBER SMOOTHIE

SERVES
2

PREP TIME
5
MINUTES

COOK TIME
/
MINUTES

- 2 ice cubes

- **1/4 cup** skim milk

- **1/4 cup** fat-free Greek Yogurt

- **1 serving** vanilla protein powder

- **1 1/2 tablespoons** unsweetened applesauce

- **1 ounce** cucumber, peeled, de-seeded and cubed

- **1/8 teaspoon** cinnamon

- Liquid stevia to taste

**1.** Blend all ingredients until smooth. Thin with water if necessary. Add Stevia to taste.

**2.** Pass the smoothie through a strainer to remove large chunks.

| CALORIES | CARBS | SUGAR | FAT | PROTEIN | SODIUM |
|---|---|---|---|---|---|
| 101 | 7.2 | 4.0 | 1.0 | 16.0 | 98 |
| KCAL | GRAMS | GRAMS | GRAMS | GRAMS | MILLIGRAMS |

# COCONUT CHAI LATTE SMOOTHIE

 **SERVES** 2

 **PREP TIME** 5 MINUTES

 **COOK TIME** / MINUTES

**1.** Blend all ingredients until smooth. Thin with water if necessary. Add Stevia to taste.

- **2 ounces** frozen skim milk cubes

- **1/4 cup** unsweetened coconut milk

- **1/4 cup** fat-free Greek Yogurt

- **1 serving** vanilla protein powder

- **1/4 teaspoon** ground cinnamon

- **1/8 teaspoon** ground ginger

- Pinch of ground cloves and ground nutmeg

- Liquid stevia to taste

| CALORIES | CARBS | SUGAR | FAT | PROTEIN | SODIUM |
|----------|-------|-------|-----|---------|--------|
| 102 | 6.3 | 3.0 | 1.6 | 15.9 | 98 |
| KCAL | GRAMS | GRAMS | GRAMS | GRAMS | MILLIGRAMS |

# FRENCH TOAST SMOOTHIE

 **SERVES**
2

 **PREP TIME**
5
MINUTES

 **COOK TIME**
/
MINUTES

- **2 ounces** frozen skim milk cubes

- **1/4 cup** skim milk

- **1/4 cup** fat-free cottage cheese

- **1 serving** vanilla protein powder

- **1/4 teaspoon** cinnamon

- **1/8 teaspoon** butter extract

- Pinch of nutmeg

- Liquid stevia to taste

**1.** Blend all ingredients until smooth. Thin with water if necessary. Add Stevia to taste.

**2.** Pass the smoothie through a strainer to remove large chunks.

| CALORIES | CARBS | SUGAR | FAT | PROTEIN | SODIUM |
|---|---|---|---|---|---|
| 116 | 7.7 | 4.5 | 0.5 | 18.8 | 200 |
| KCAL | GRAMS | GRAMS | GRAMS | GRAMS | MILLIGRAMS |

# BANANA TOFU SMOOTHIE

 **SERVES**
2

 **PREP TIME**
5
MINUTES

 **COOK TIME**
/
MINUTES

1. Blend all ingredients until smooth. Thin with water if necessary. Add Stevia to taste.

2. Pass the smoothie through a strainer to remove large chunks.

- **2 ounces** ice cubes

- **4 ounces** silken tofu

- **1 serving** vanilla protein powder

- **2 ounces** very ripe banana

- **1/4 teaspoon** cinnamon

- Liquid stevia to taste

| CALORIES | CARBS | SUGAR | FAT | PROTEIN | SODIUM |
|---|---|---|---|---|---|
| 142 | 11.2 | 3.9 | 3.1 | 19.3 | 75 |
| KCAL | GRAMS | GRAMS | GRAMS | GRAMS | MILLIGRAMS |

# TUMERIC YOGURT SMOOTHIE

 SERVES
2

 PREP TIME
5
MINUTES

 COOK TIME
/
MINUTES

- **2 ounces** frozen skim milk cubes

- **1/4 cup** skim milk

- **1/2 cup** fat-free Greek Yogurt

- **1 serving** vanilla protein powder

- **1/2 teaspoon** ground turmeric

- Liquid stevia to taste

**1.** Blend all ingredients until smooth. Thin with water if necessary. Add Stevia to taste.

**2.** Pass the smoothie through a strainer to remove large chunks.

| CALORIES | CARBS | SUGAR | FAT | PROTEIN | SODIUM |
|----------|-------|-------|-----|---------|--------|
| 117 | 8.1 | 4.8 | 1.1 | 18.8 | 117 |
| KCAL | GRAMS | GRAMS | GRAMS | GRAMS | MILLIGRAMS |

# APPLE COTTAGE CHEESE SMOOTHIE

**SERVES**
2

**PREP TIME**
5
MINUTES

**COOK TIME**
/
MINUTES

1. Blend all ingredients until smooth. Thin with water if necessary. Add Stevia to taste.

2. Pass the smoothie through a strainer to remove large chunks.

- **2 ounces** ice cubes

- **1/4 cup** water

- **1/4 cup** fat-free Cottage Cheese

- **1 serving** vanilla protein powder

- **1/4 cup** unsweetened apple sauce

- **1/8 teaspoon** cinnamon

- Pinch of nutmeg

- Liquid stevia to taste

| CALORIES | CARBS | SUGAR | FAT | PROTEIN | SODIUM |
|----------|-------|-------|-----|---------|--------|
| 106 | 7.8 | 4.2 | 1.0 | 16.8 | 178 |
| KCAL | GRAMS | GRAMS | GRAMS | GRAMS | MILLIGRAMS |

# BLACK BEAN CHOCOLATE SMOOTHIE

 **SERVES**
2

 **PREP TIME**
5
MINUTES

 **COOK TIME**
/
MINUTES

- **2 ounces** ice cubes

- **1/2 cup** skim milk

- **1/4 cup** canned black beans, rinsed and drained

- **1 serving** vanilla protein powder

- **1 tablespoon** unsweetened cocoa powder

- Liquid stevia to taste

**1.** Blend all ingredients until smooth. Thin with water if necessary. Add Stevia to taste.

**2.** Pass the smoothie through a strainer to remove large chunks.

| CALORIES | CARBS | SUGAR | FAT | PROTEIN | SODIUM |
|----------|-------|-------|-----|---------|--------|
| 126 | 12.6 | 3.8 | 1.5 | 17.3 | 103 |
| KCAL | GRAMS | GRAMS | GRAMS | GRAMS | MILLIGRAMS |

# GINGERBREAD AND BEAN SMOOTHIE

 **SERVES**
2

 **PREP TIME**
5
MINUTES

 **COOK TIME**
/
MINUTES

1. Blend all ingredients until smooth. Thin with water if necessary. Add Stevia to taste.

2. Pass the smoothie through a strainer to remove large chunks.

- **2 ounces** frozen skim milk cubes

- **1/4 cup** skim milk

- **1/4 cup** canned pinto beans, rinsed and drained

- **1 serving** vanilla protein powder

- **1 tablespoon** fresh ginger juice

- **1/4 teaspoon** cinnamon

- Pinch of ground cloves and nutmeg

- Liquid stevia to taste

| CALORIES | CARBS | SUGAR | FAT | PROTEIN | SODIUM |
|----------|-------|-------|-----|---------|--------|
| 127 | 12.3 | 3.9 | 1.3 | 16.6 | 192 |
| KCAL | GRAMS | GRAMS | GRAMS | GRAMS | MILLIGRAMS |

# PUMPKIN PIE SMOOTHIE

SERVES
2

PREP TIME
5
MINUTES

COOK TIME
/
MINUTES

- **2 ounces** frozen skim milk cubes

- **1/4 cup** skim milk

- **1/4 cup** canned white beans, rinsed and drained

- **1 serving** vanilla protein powder

- **1/4 cup** canned pumpkin

- **1/4 teaspoon** cinnamon

- **1/8 teaspoon** nutmeg

- Liquid stevia to taste

1. Blend all ingredients until smooth. Thin with water if necessary. Add Stevia to taste.

2. Pass the smoothie through a strainer to remove large chunks.

| CALORIES | CARBS | SUGAR | FAT | PROTEIN | SODIUM |
|----------|-------|-------|-----|---------|--------|
| 134 | 14.1 | 4.8 | 1.2 | 17.0 | 169 |
| KCAL | GRAMS | GRAMS | GRAMS | GRAMS | MILLIGRAMS |

# GINGER BEET TOFU SMOOTHIE

 SERVES
2

 PREP TIME
10
MINUTES

 COOK TIME
/
MINUTES

1. Blend all ingredients until smooth. Thin with water if necessary. Add Stevia to taste.

2. Pass the puree through a strainer to remove large chunks.

- **2 ounces** ice cubes

- **1/4 cup** skim milk

- **2 ounces** silken tofu

- **1 serving** vanilla protein powder

- **2 ounces** cooked beet

- **1 tablespoon** fresh ginger juice

- Liquid stevia to taste

| CALORIES | CARBS | SUGAR | FAT | PROTEIN | SODIUM |
|---|---|---|---|---|---|
| 125 | 9.9 | 4.7 | 2.1 | 17.6 | 112 |
| KCAL | GRAMS | GRAMS | GRAMS | GRAMS | MILLIGRAMS |

# LIME AND KALE SMOOTHIE

 **SERVES**
**2**

 **PREP TIME**
**10**
MINUTES

 **COOK TIME**
**/**
MINUTES

- **2 ounces** frozen skim milk cubes

- **1/4 cup** skim milk

- **1/4 cup** fat-free Greek Yogurt

- **1 serving** vanilla protein powder

- **1/4 cup** cooked kale

- **1 tablespoons** Lime Juice

- Liquid stevia to taste

**1.** Blend all ingredients until smooth. Thin with water if necessary. Add Stevia to taste.

**2.** Pass the smoothie through a strainer to remove large chunks.

| CALORIES | CARBS | SUGAR | FAT | PROTEIN | SODIUM |
|----------|-------|-------|-----|---------|--------|
| 111 | 8.6 | 4.6 | 1.1 | 17.2 | 113 |
| KCAL | GRAMS | GRAMS | GRAMS | GRAMS | MILLIGRAMS |

# PUMPKIN CHAI MOUSSE

 **SERVES**
3

 **PREP TIME**
5
MINUTES

 **COOK TIME**
/
MINUTES

1. Blend all ingredients until smooth. Thin with water if necessary. Add Stevia to taste.

2. Pass the puree through a strainer to remove large chunks.

- **1 cup** fat-free cottage cheese

- **1/2 cup** canned pumpkin

- **1/2 teaspoon** vanilla extract

- **1/4 teaspoon** cinnamon

- **1/8 teaspoon** nutmeg

- Pinch of turmeric and salt

| CALORIES | CARBS | SUGAR | FAT | PROTEIN | SODIUM |
|---|---|---|---|---|---|
| 70 | 6.9 | 3.4 | 0.2 | 10.5 | 262 |
| KCAL | GRAMS | GRAMS | GRAMS | GRAMS | MILLIGRAMS |

# PURPLE YAM MOUSSE

 **SERVES** **3**

 **PREP TIME** **15** MINUTES

 **COOK TIME** **5** MINUTES

- **4 ounces** purple yam, peeled and cooked

- **1/2 cup** fat-free cottage cheese

- **1/4 cup** fat-free half-and half

- **1/2 serving** vanilla protein powder

- **1/4 teaspoon** vanilla extract

- liquid stevia to taste

1. Blend all ingredients until smooth. Thin with water if necessary. Add Stevia to taste.

2. Pass the mousse through a strainer to remove large chunks.

| CALORIES | CARBS | SUGAR | FAT | PROTEIN | SODIUM |
|---|---|---|---|---|---|
| 108 | 14.4 | 3.7 | 0.6 | 10.5 | 175 |
| KCAL | GRAMS | GRAMS | GRAMS | GRAMS | MILLIGRAMS |

# CREAMY RED BEAN POPSICLE

SERVES
**6**

PREP TIME
**6**
HOURS

COOK TIME
**/**
MINUTES

**1.** Blend all ingredients until smooth. Thin with water if necessary. Add Stevia to taste.

**2.** Pass the puree through a strainer to remove large chunks.

**3.** Divide the mixture into 6 4-ounce popsicle mold. Insert the stick and refrigerate for 6 hours.

- **1 1/4 cups** canned red beans, rinsed and drained

- **3/4 cup** skim milk

- **1/2 cup** fat-free half and half

- **1 1/2 servings** vanilla protein powder

- pinch of kosher salt

- liquid stevia to taste

| CALORIES | CARBS | SUGAR | FAT | PROTEIN | SODIUM |
|----------|-------|-------|-----|---------|--------|
| 103 | 12.3 | 2.8 | 0.6 | 11.1 | 144 |
| KCAL | GRAMS | GRAMS | GRAMS | GRAMS | MILLIGRAMS |

# BEEF AND VEGETABLES STIR FRY

 **SERVES** **8**

 **PREP TIME** **15** MINUTES

 **COOK TIME** **10** MINUTES

- **1 pound** lean flank steak, cut into strips

- **1/4 cup** fat-free beef broth

- **2 cups** broccoli florets

- **1 cup** sliced bell peppers

- **1 cup** sliced carrot

- **1** green onion, chopped

- **2 cloves** garlic, minced

- **2 tablespoons** low sodium soy sauce

- **1 tablespoon** grated ginger

- **1 teaspoon** stevia

1. In a small bowl, mix beef with soy sauce, stevia and ginger. Set aside to marinate for 10 minutes.

2. Spray a large skillet. Sauté the onion until fragrant. Then add all the vegetables. Cook for 4-5 minutes until vegetables are tender. Remove from the skillet.

3. Add the beef. Reserve the marinade. Cook until the beef is brown. Then return the vegetables, broth and marinade. Stir and cook for 2 minutes.

| CALORIES | CARBS | SUGAR | FAT | PROTEIN | SODIUM |
|---|---|---|---|---|---|
| 99 | 4.6 | 1.9 | 2.6 | 13.4 | 337 |
| KCAL | GRAMS | GRAMS | GRAMS | GRAMS | MILLIGRAMS |

# THAI GROUND BEEF

 **SERVES** 8

 **PREP TIME** 10 MINUTES

 **COOK TIME** 20 MINUTES

**1.** Spray a large skillet.

**2.** Sauté the leek until fragrant. Then add garlic and sauté for 1 more minute.

**3.** Brown the beef.

**4.** Stir in curry paste and tomato sauce. Simmer for 3-4 minutes or until the liquid is reduced to half.

**5.** Stir in the coconut milk and seasoning. Bring to a boil. Serve immediately.

- **1 pound** 95/5 lean ground beef
- **2 cloves** garlic, minced
- **1 cup** thinly sliced leek
- **1 cup** no-sugar-added tomato sauce
- **1/2 cup** light coconut milk
- **1 tablespoon** red curry paste
- **1/2 tablespoon** stevia
- **1/2 tablespoon** fish sauce
- **1/2 tablespoon** lime juice
- **1/2 teaspoon** Sriracha sauce (optional)
- **1/4 teaspoon** lime zest
- salt and pepper to taste
- Nonstick Cooking Spray

| CALORIES | CARBS | SUGAR | FAT | PROTEIN | SODIUM |
|----------|-------|-------|-----|---------|--------|
| 106 | 4.1 | 2.1 | 3.9 | 13.0 | 270 |
| KCAL | GRAMS | GRAMS | GRAMS | GRAMS | MILLIGRAMS |

# SPICY BEEF WITH BOK CHOY

 **SERVES**
**8**

 **PREP TIME**
**15**
MINUTES

 **COOK TIME**
**20**
MINUTES

- **1 pound** lean flank steak, cut into strips
- **6 heads** baby Bok Choy, cut in half
- **1 cup** sliced onion
- **2 cloves** garlic, minced
- **2** chili peppers, deseeded and chopped
- **1 tablespoon** grated ginger
- 2 tablespoons fish sauce
- 1/4 teaspoon salt
- 1/4 teaspoon pepper
- Nonstick Cooking Spray

1. In a medium bowl, season the beef with salt and pepper.

2. Sauté the garlic, ginger and chili until fragrant. Add the beef and cook for 3 minutes. Set Aside.

3. Sauté the onion until fragrant.

4. Then add Bok Choy and cook until soft.

5. Add the beef and fish sauce. Mix well and cook for 1 minute.

| CALORIES | CARBS | SUGAR | FAT | PROTEIN | SODIUM |
|----------|-------|-------|-----|---------|--------|
| 114 | 5.7 | 1.6 | 2.6 | 13.5 | 469 |
| KCAL | GRAMS | GRAMS | GRAMS | GRAMS | MILLIGRAMS |

# BEEF STUFFED BELL PEPPER

 **SERVES**
8

 **PREP TIME**
5
MINUTES

 **COOK TIME**
35
MINUTES

1. Preheat the oven to 375°F.

2. Spray a large skillet.

3. Sauté the onion until fragrant. Then add garlic, green onion

4. and green peppers. Sauté for 3 more minutes. Set aside.

5. Brown the beef. Then all ingredients except cheese and tomato sauce. Mix well and cook for another 5 minutes.

6. Fill the bell peppers half the way with the meat mixture. Add cheddar cheese. Then add the remaining meat mixture. Top with tomato sauce and mozzarella cheese.

7. Bake for 20-25 minutes.

- **1 pound** 95/5 lean ground beef
- **4** medium green bell peppers, tops and seeds removed
- **1 cup** canned diced tomatoes
- **1/3 cup** finely chopped onion
- **1/4 cup** finely chopped green onion
- **1/4 cup** fat-free mozzarella cheese
- **1/4 cup** fat-free cheddar cheese
- **1/2 cup** no-sugar-added tomato and pesto sauce
- **2 cloves** garlic, minced
- **2 tablespoons** minced green peppers
- **2 tablespoons** chopped fresh parsley
- **1 1/2 teaspoons** Italian seasoning
- 1 teaspoon salt
- **1/2 teaspoon** ground black pepper
- Nonstick Cooking Spray

| CALORIES | CARBS | SUGAR | FAT | PROTEIN | SODIUM |
|---|---|---|---|---|---|
| 118 | 7.7 | 3.6 | 3.2 | 15.6 | 471 |
| KCAL | GRAMS | GRAMS | GRAMS | GRAMS | MILLIGRAMS |

# SALISBURY STEAK WITH MUSHROOM SAUCE

 **SERVES**
8

 **PREP TIME**
15
MINUTES

 **COOK TIME**
25
MINUTES

## For the Salisbury Steak

- **1 pound** 95/5 lean ground beef
- **1/4 cup** whole wheat bread crumbs
- **1/4 cup** chopped onion
- **2 egg whites**, beaten
- **1 teaspoon** salt
- Nonstick Cooking Spray

## For the Gravy

- **2 cups** fat-free beef broth
- **1 1/2 cups** sliced onion
- **1 cup** sliced mushrooms
- **2 tablespoons** whole wheat flour
- salt and pepper to taste

**1.** Combine all ingredients for the steak. Shape into 8 mini patties.

**2.** Spray a large skillet. Brown the Steak on both sides over medium heat, about 4-5 minutes each side.

**3.** Add broth, onion and mushroom. Bring to a boil then reduce to low. Cover and simmer for 10 more minutes. Transfer the patties to the serving plate.

**4.** In a small bowl, combine flour with a few tablespoons of water. Then slowly stir in the mixture. Cook until sauce thickened. Pour the sauce on the steak and serve.

| CALORIES | CARBS | SUGAR | FAT | PROTEIN | SODIUM |
|---|---|---|---|---|---|
| 120 | 50 | 0.9 | 2.9 | 17.0 | 566 |
| KCAL | GRAMS | GRAMS | GRAMS | GRAMS | MILLIGRAMS |

# MEXICAN BEEF SKILLET

SERVES
8

PREP TIME
10
MINUTES

COOK TIME
35
MINUTES

1. In a medium bowl, season the beef with chili powder, salt and paprika.

2. Spray a large skillet, cook the beef for 3 minutes. Set aside.

3. Sauté the garlic, onion and bell peppers until fragrant. Then add mushroom and cook for another 2 minutes.

4. Add broth and salsa. Simmer until the liquid is reduced by half. Stir in beef and cook for 1 minute.

- **1 pound** lean flank steak, cut into strips

- **1 cup** sliced onion

- **1 cup** sliced mushroom

- **1 cup** sliced red bell pepper

- **3/4 cup** fat-free low sodium chicken broth

- **1/2 cup** no-sugar-added salsa

- **2 cloves** garlic, minced

- **2 teaspoons** chili powder

- 1 teaspoon paprika

- 1/2 teaspoon salt

- Nonstick Cooking Spray

| CALORIES | CARBS | SUGAR | FAT | PROTEIN | SODIUM |
|----------|-------|-------|-----|---------|--------|
| 102 | 4.4 | 1.9 | 2.7 | 13.2 | 339 |
| KCAL | GRAMS | GRAMS | GRAMS | GRAMS | MILLIGRAMS |

# INDIAN BEEF CURRY

**SERVES**
8

**PREP TIME**
10
MINUTES

**COOK TIME**
40
MINUTES

- **1 pound** 95/5 lean ground beef
- **1** 14.5-ounce **can** diced tomatoes
- **1 cup** chopped onion
- **1/2 cup** frozen peas, thawed
- **1 cup** fat-free beef broth
- **1/2 cup** fat-free Greek Yogurt
- **2 cloves** garlic, minced
- **2 tablespoons** curry powder
- **1/2 teaspoon** chili paste
- **1/4 teaspoon** ground turmeric
- salt to taste
- **2 tablespoons** chopped fresh Parsley

1. Spray a large skillet.

2. Sauté the onion until fragrant. Then add garlic and sauté for 1 more minute.

3. Brown the beef. Transfer the beef mixture to a bowl.

4. Add turmeric, curry powder and chili paste. Cook for 30 seconds.

5. Slowly stir in broth and tomatoes. Add Peas. Bring to a boil. Simmer for 15 minutes or until the peas soften.

6. Add beef mixture back. Season with salt.

7. Remove from heat. Stir in yogurt and sprinkle with chopped parsley.

| CALORIES | CARBS | SUGAR | FAT | PROTEIN | SODIUM |
|----------|-------|-------|-----|---------|--------|
| 113 | 6.4 | 2.9 | 3.3 | 15.0 | 316 |
| KCAL | GRAMS | GRAMS | GRAMS | GRAMS | MILLIGRAMS |

# SKINNY ENCHILADAS

 **SERVES**
9

 **PREP TIME**
10
MINUTES

 **COOK TIME**
45
MINUTES

**1.** Preheat the oven to 350°F

**2.** Spray a large skillet.

**3.** Sauté the onion until fragrant. Then Brown the beef. Season with salt and pepper.

**4.** In a large bowl, combine yogurt, soup and half of the cheese.

**5.** Mix half of the soup mixture with the meat. Divide the meat between tortillas. Roll up and place them in a baking dish. Top with the remaining sauce and cheese.

**6.** Bake for 30 minutes.

- **1 pound** 95/5 lean ground beef
- **3** low carb tortillas
- 1 10.5-ounce **can** condensed 98% fat-free cream of chicken soup
- **1/2 cup** chopped green onions
- **1/2 cup** fat-free Greek yogurt
- **1 1/2 cups** fat-free mozzarella cheese
- **1** jalapeno pepper, de-seeded and chopped
- **2 tablespoons** Taco seasoning
- salt and pepper to taste

| CALORIES | CARBS | SUGAR | FAT | PROTEIN | SODIUM |
|----------|-------|-------|-----|---------|--------|
| 149 | 7.5 | 0.6 | 4.3 | 19.9 | 495 |
| KCAL | GRAMS | GRAMS | GRAMS | GRAMS | MILLIGRAMS |

# BEEF CHILI

 **SERVES**
**8**

 **PREP TIME**
**10**
MINUTES

 **COOK TIME**
**60**
MINUTES

- **1 pound** 95/5 lean ground beef

- **1** 15-ounce **can** dark red kidney beans, rinsed and drained

- **1/2 cup** chopped onion

- **1 1/2 cups** no-sugar-added tomato juice

- **1/2 cup** no-sugar-added salsa

- **1 tablespoon** chili powder

- **1/2 tablespoon** garlic powde

- **1/2 teaspoon** ground cumin

- **1/2 teaspoon** paprika

- **1/4 teaspoon** thyme

**1.** Spray a large skillet.

**2.** Sauté the onion until fragrant. Then Brown the beef.

**3.** Add all ingredients and mix well. Bring to a boil. Reduce to low and simmer for 50 minutes. Season with salt and pepper.

| CALORIES | CARBS | SUGAR | FAT | PROTEIN | SODIUM |
|---|---|---|---|---|---|
| 147 | 14.6 | 3.7 | 3.3 | 15.7 | 227 |
| KCAL | GRAMS | GRAMS | GRAMS | GRAMS | MILLIGRAMS |

# CHEESE-STUFFED MEATLOAF

**SERVES**
**8**

**PREP TIME**
**20**
MINUTES

**COOK TIME**
**60**
MINUTES

1. Preheat the oven to 350°F

2. In a large mixing bowl, combine all ingredients except cheese.

3. Spread the meat mixture on a large baking sheet to form a 14"x18" patty.

4. Add the cheese on the meat. Leave out 1-inch on each side.

5. Roll up and Put it in a 10"x15" baking dish.

6. Bake for 1 hour.

- **2 pounds** 95/5 lean ground beef

- **1/2 cup** whole wheat breadcrumbs

- **1/2 cup** chopped onion

- **4 egg whites**, beaten

- **2 cups** fat-free shredded cheddar cheese

- **1 1/2 teaspoons** salt

- **1 1/2 teaspoons** ground black pepper

| CALORIES | CARBS | SUGAR | FAT | PROTEIN | SODIUM |
|----------|-------|-------|-----|---------|--------|
| 83 | 3.6 | 0.5 | 1.6 | 13.7 | 412 |
| KCAL | GRAMS | GRAMS | GRAMS | GRAMS | MILLIGRAMS |

# ITALIAN PARMESAN MEATBALLS

 **SERVES** 8

 **PREP TIME** 20 MINUTES

 **COOK TIME** 70 MINUTES

- **1 pound** 95/5 lean ground beef
- **1/4 cup** whole wheat breadcrumbs
- **1/4 cup** fat-free shredded Parmesan Cheese
- **1/4 cup** fat-free shredded mozzarella cheese
- **1 1/4 cups** No-sugar-added tomato and basil sauce
- **1 1/2 tablespoons** Italian Seasoning
- **1/2 teaspoon** salt
- **1/2 teaspoon** ground black pepper
- **2 tablespoons** chopped fresh parsley

1. Preheat the oven to 350°F

2. In a large mixing bowl, combine beef, breadcrumbs, parmesan cheese, 1/4 cup of the tomato sauce and seasoning. Shape into 8 meatballs.

3. Bake for 15 minutes.

4. On an oven-proof skillet, add the remaining sauce and the meatballs. Toss well. Top with the mozzarella cheese and bake to another 15 minutes. Sprinkle with parsley before serving.

| CALORIES | CARBS | SUGAR | FAT | PROTEIN | SODIUM |
|---|---|---|---|---|---|
| 116 KCAL | 6.7 GRAMS | 1.9 GRAMS | 3.4 GRAMS | 14.7 GRAMS | 454 MILLIGRAMS |

# CABBAGE AND BEEF BAKE

 **SERVES**
**12**

 **PREP TIME**
**15**
MINUTES

 **COOK TIME**
**80**
MINUTES

1. Preheat the oven to 350°F

2. Spray a large skillet.

3. Sauté the onion and bell peppers until fragrant. Then Brown the beef. Stir in Tomatoes. Season with salt and pepper Set aside.

4. Spray a 9"x13" baking dish. Spread the shredded cabbage evenly. Then spread the meat mixture on top.

5. In a small bowl, mix together tomato sauce and sour cream. Then spread the mixture on the meat.

6. Bake for 1 hour. Then top with cheese and bake for another 20 minutes.

- **1 1/2 pounds** 95/5 lean ground beef

- **6 cups** shredded cabbage

- **1 cup** chopped onion

- **1/2 cup** chopped bell peppers

- 1 14.5-ounce **can** diced tomato

- 1 8-ounce **can** tomato sauce

- **1 cup** fat-free sour cream

- **1/2 cup** fat-free shredded cheddar cheese

- **1/2 cup** fat-free shredded mozzarella cheese

- salt and pepper to taste

| CALORIES | CARBS | SUGAR | FAT | PROTEIN | SODIUM |
|---|---|---|---|---|---|
| 131 | 9.0 | 4.8 | 3.1 | 17.6 | 313 |
| KCAL | GRAMS | GRAMS | GRAMS | GRAMS | MILLIGRAMS |

# BEER BRAISED BEEF

 **SERVES**
16

 **PREP TIME**
5
MINUTES

 **COOK TIME**
3
HOURS

- **2 pounds** lean top round roast
- **2 cans** beer
- **2** large onion, sliced
- **4 cloves** garlic
- **1 teaspoon** salt
- **1 teaspoon** Ground Thyme
- **1/2 teaspoon** Rosemary
- **1/2 teaspoon** ground black pepper
- Nonstick cooking spray

1. Preheat the oven to 275°F

2. Spray a large Dutch oven. Sauté the onion until fragrant. Set aside.

3. Season the meat with salt and pepper. Brown the meat on all side for about 2 minutes per side. Add all ingredients.

4. Cover and cook in the oven for 2 3/4 to 3 hours.

5. Shred the meat with a pair of forks before serving.

| CALORIES | CARBS | SUGAR | FAT | PROTEIN | SODIUM |
|---|---|---|---|---|---|
| 96 | 3.6 | 0.8 | 2.0 | 13.0 | 247 |
| KCAL | GRAMS | GRAMS | GRAMS | GRAMS | MILLIGRAMS |

# SICHUAN SPICY BEEF STEW

 **SERVES**
16

 **PREP TIME**
15
MINUTES

 **COOK TIME**
2
HOURS

1. Blanch the beef in boiling water. Drain and set aside.

2. Spray a wok. Sauté the ginger and garlic until fragrant. Add the chili paste and cook for 30 seconds.

3. Add beef, soy sauce and wine. Stir well and cook for 2 minutes.

4. Transfer to a stock pot. Add the spices and enough water to cover the beef. Bring to a boil and reduce to low. Simmer for 1 hour.

5. Add Radish. Cook for another 30 minutes or until both beef and radish are tender. Garnish with cilantro and serve.

- **2 pounds** lean top round roast, cut into 1 1/2 slices across the grain
- **1 pound** radish, cut into 2-inch pieces
- **5 cloves** garlic, minced
- **4 slices** fresh ginger
- **3 tablespoons** dry white wine
- **2 tablespoons** chopped fresh cilantro
- **1 tablespoon** Sichuan chilli bean paste
- **1 tablespoon** low-sodium soy sauce
- Nonstick Cooking Spray

<u>Spices:</u>

- **4** dried chili
- **2** star anise
- **2** bay leaves
- **1** cinnamon stick
- **1 teaspoon** peppercorn
- **1 teaspoon** fennel seeds

| CALORIES | CARBS | SUGAR | FAT | PROTEIN | SODIUM |
|---|---|---|---|---|---|
| 84 | 2.4 | 0.7 | 2.0 | 13.0 | 102 |
| KCAL | GRAMS | GRAMS | GRAMS | GRAMS | MILLIGRAMS |

# MONGOLIAN BEEF SKEWER

SERVES
8

PREP TIME
8
HOURS

COOK TIME
10
MINUTES

- **1 pound** lean flank steak, cut into strips

- **2 tablespoons** low-sodium soy sauce

- **2 tablespoons** sherry cooking wine

- **1 tablespoon** grated ginger

- **1 tablespoon** minced garlic

- **2 teaspoons** Truvia Nectar

- **1 teaspoon** dried mustard powder

**1.** In a large resealable bag, add all ingredients. Seal and shake the bag to mix well. Marinate overnight.

**2.** Preheat the broiler. Thread the meat onto 16 skewers.

**3.** Broil 3-4 minutes on each side.

| CALORIES | CARBS | SUGAR | FAT | PROTEIN | SODIUM |
|----------|-------|-------|-----|---------|--------|
| 90 | 1.8 | 1.0 | 2.6 | 12.3 | 210 |
| KCAL | GRAMS | GRAMS | GRAMS | GRAMS | MILLIGRAMS |

# CHICKEN AND SUGAR SNAP PEA STIR FRY

 SERVES
8

 PREP TIME
10
MINUTES

 COOK TIME
15
MINUTES

**1.** Spray a large skillet. Brown the chicken. Add oyster sauce and cook for another minute. Set aside.

**2.** Sauté green onion and garlic until fragrant. Then add peas and cook until fragrant. Stir in chicken and stir-fry for 30 seconds.

- **1 pound** chicken tender, cut into strips

- **12 ounces** sugar snap peas, , cut into strips

- **1 tablespoon** oyster sauce

- **2 cloves** garlic, minced

- **2** green onions, chopped

- salt and pepper to taste

| CALORIES | CARBS | SUGAR | FAT | PROTEIN | SODIUM |
|----------|-------|-------|-----|---------|--------|
| 59 | 1.7 | 0.6 | 0.3 | 11.5 | 118 |
| KCAL | GRAMS | GRAMS | GRAMS | GRAMS | MILLIGRAMS |

# LEMON THYME CHICKEN

 SERVES
8

 PREP TIME
15
MINUTES

 COOK TIME
20
MINUTES

- **1 pound** chicken tender

- **1/4 cup** lemon juice

- **6 sprigs** fresh thyme, chopped

- **1 tablespoon** lemon zest

- **2 cloves** garlic, minced

- salt and pepper to taste

- Nonstick Cooking Spray

1. In a large bowl, mix the chicken in all other ingredients. Set aside to marinate for 15 minutes.

2. Spray a large skillet. Cook the chicken until cook through, about 4-5 minutes each side

| CALORIES | CARBS | SUGAR | FAT | PROTEIN | SODIUM |
|----------|-------|-------|-----|---------|--------|
| 55 | 1.0 | 0.2 | 0.2 | 11.3 | 56 |
| KCAL | GRAMS | GRAMS | GRAMS | GRAMS | MILLIGRAMS |

# PEPPER-STUFFED CAJUN CHICKEN

 **SERVES**
8

 **PREP TIME**
10
MINUTES

 **COOK TIME**
25
MINUTES

**1.** Preheat the oven to 350°F.

**2.** Spray a large skillet.

**3.** Sauté the onion and bell peppers until fragrant. Season with salt and pepper. Set aside to cool.

**4.** Slice the chicken breast to form a pocket. Stuff the vegetable and then the cheese.

**5.** Rub the Cajun seasoning, then salt and pepper on all side of the chicken breast.

**6.** Bake for 25 minutes

- **4** boneless, skinless chicken breast
- **1 cup** chopped onion
- **1 cup** chopped bell peppers
- **1 cup** fat free cheddar cheese
- **1 tablespoon** Cajun seasoning
- salt and pepper to taste
- Nonstick Cooking Spray

| CALORIES | CARBS | SUGAR | FAT | PROTEIN | SODIUM |
|---|---|---|---|---|---|
| 91 | 4.0 | 1.6 | 0.6 | 16.3 | 522 |
| KCAL | GRAMS | GRAMS | GRAMS | GRAMS | MILLIGRAMS |

# SPINACH FETA CHICKEN ROLL

 **SERVES**
**8**

 **PREP TIME**
**10**
MINUTES

 **COOK TIME**
**25**
MINUTES

- **4** boneless, skinless chicken breast, flattened
- **10 ounces** frozen spinach, thawed and squeeze
- **1/2 cup** fat-free feta cheese
- **1/3 cup** fat-free ricotta cheese
- **1/4 cup** chopped green onion
- **1/4 cup** chopped fresh parsley
- **1 tablespoon** fresh dill
- **2 cloves** garlic
- salt and pepper to taste

**1.** Preheat the oven to 350°F.

**2.** Spray a large skillet.

**3.** Sauté the green onion and garlic until fragrant. Add spinach, parsley and dill. Cool until heated through. Season with salt and pepper.

**4.** Remove from heat and stir in feta cheese and ricotta cheese.

**5.** Divide the mixture onto the chicken breast. Roll up. Rub the chicken with salt and pepper.

**6.** Bake for 25 minutes.

| CALORIES | CARBS | SUGAR | FAT | PROTEIN | SODIUM |
|----------|-------|-------|-----|---------|--------|
| 83 | 2.1 | 0.8 | 0.6 | 15.0 | 328 |
| KCAL | GRAMS | GRAMS | GRAMS | GRAMS | MILLIGRAMS |

# CREAMY SALSA CHICKEN

 **SERVES**
**8**

 **PREP TIME**
**5**
MINUTES

 **COOK TIME**
**35**
MINUTES

**1.** Preheat the oven to 350°F.

**2.** Season the chicken with half of the taco seasoning.

**3.** Brown the chicken in an -oven-proof skillet. Then stir in salsa and the remaining seasoning.

**4.** Cover and bake for 30 minutes.

**5.** Shred the chicken and stir in sour cream.

- **1 pound** chicken tender
- **2 cups** salsa
- **1 package** taco seasoning
- **1 cup** fat-free soup cream
- Nonstick Cooking Spray

| CALORIES | CARBS | SUGAR | FAT | PROTEIN | SODIUM |
|----------|-------|-------|-----|---------|--------|
| 92 | 5.5 | 4.0 | 0.2 | 12.0 | 296 |
| KCAL | GRAMS | GRAMS | GRAMS | GRAMS | MILLIGRAMS |

# YOGURT CHICKEN PARMESAN

 **SERVES** 8

 **PREP TIME** 10 MINUTES

 **COOK TIME** 45 MINUTES

- **1 pound** chicken tender

- **1/2 cup** fat-free Greek Yogurt

- **1/2 cup** low-fat mayonnaise

- **1/2 cup** fat-free grated parmesan cheese

- **1/2 teaspoon** salt

- **1/2 teaspoon** ground black pepper

1. Preheat the oven to 375°F.

2. In a medium bowl, mix yogurt, mayonnaise, cheese and seasonings.

3. Line the chicken on a baking tray. Spread the mixture on the chicken breast.

4. Bake for 45 minutes.

| CALORIES | CARBS | SUGAR | FAT | PROTEIN | SODIUM |
|----------|-------|-------|-----|---------|--------|
| 88 | 5.6 | 1.4 | 1.2 | 13.4 | 463 |
| KCAL | GRAMS | GRAMS | GRAMS | GRAMS | MILLIGRAMS |

# HUNGARIAN CHICKEN PAPRIKASH

SERVES
8

PREP TIME
10
MINUTES

COOK TIME
50
MINUTES

1. Season the chicken with salt and pepper. Spray a large skillet. Brown the chicken. Set aside.

2. Sauté the onion until fragrant. Add paprika and cook for 2 minutes. Add broth, tomato and chicken. Bring to a boil then reduce to low. Cover and simmer for 30 minutes.

3. Remove from heat and stir in sour cream before serving.

- **1 pound** chicken tender

- **1 cup** chopped onion

- **2** plum tomatoes, cubed

- **1 cup** fat-free low sodium chicken broth

- **1/4 cup** fat free sour cream

- **1 tablespoon** sweet paprika

- **1 teaspoon** smoked paprika

- salt and pepper to taste

| CALORIES | CARBS | SUGAR | FAT | PROTEIN | SODIUM |
|---|---|---|---|---|---|
| 72 | 3.7 | 1.9 | 0.4 | 12.2 | 80 |
| KCAL | GRAMS | GRAMS | GRAMS | GRAMS | MILLIGRAMS |

# ROSEMARY BRAISED CHICKEN

 **SERVES**
8

 **PREP TIME**
5
MINUTES

 **COOK TIME**
55
MINUTES

- **1 pound** chicken tender

- **1 cup** white wine

- **3 sprigs** fresh rosemary

- **2** bay leave

- **1** lemon, juice only

- salt and pepper to taste

1. Preheat the oven to 375°F.

2. Season the chicken with salt and pepper.

3. In an oven-proof skillet, Brown the chicken. Add wine and herbs. Cook until the sauce reduces by half. Then add 1 1/2 cups water and bring to a boil.

4. Cover and bake for 45 minutes. Stir in lemon juice before serving.

| CALORIES | CARBS | SUGAR | FAT | PROTEIN | SODIUM |
|---|---|---|---|---|---|
| 81 | 1.2 | 0.5 | 0.3 | 11.0 | 57 |
| KCAL | GRAMS | GRAMS | GRAMS | GRAMS | MILLIGRAMS |

# INDONESIAN COCONUT CHICKEN OPOR

 **SERVES**
8

 **PREP TIME**
5
MINUTES

 **COOK TIME**
60
MINUTES

1. Blend all ingredients for the opor paste except lemongrass until smooth.

2. Brown the chicken. Then Brown the Tofu. Set aside.

3. Sauté the paste for 1 minute. Then add all ingredients except coconut milk. Add 4 cups of water. Bring to a boil then reduce to low. Cover and simmer for 45 minutes or until chicken is tender.

4. Stir in coconut milk and simmer, uncovered, for another 10 minutes.

## Main Ingredients

- 1 pound chicken tender
- 10 ounce firm tofu, cut into bite-size pieces
- 1 1/2 cups light coconut milk
- 1/2 cups low sodium chicken broth
- Nonstick Cooking Spray

## Opor Paste

- 10 shallots
- 10 cloves garlic
- 3 fresh bay leaves
- 2 lemongrass
- 1 tablespoon freshly grated ginger
- 2 teaspoons coriander powder
- 1 teaspoon ground turmeric
- 1/2 teaspoon salt
- 1/4 teaspoon pepper

| CALORIES | CARBS | SUGAR | FAT | PROTEIN | SODIUM |
|----------|-------|-------|-----|---------|--------|
| 136 | 9.0 | 1.1 | 4.1 | 15.5 | 226 |
| KCAL | GRAMS | GRAMS | GRAMS | GRAMS | MILLIGRAMS |

# ITALIAN STUFFED CHICKEN BREAST

 **SERVES**
**8**

 **PREP TIME**
**20**
MINUTES

 **COOK TIME**
**45**
MINUTES

- **4** boneless, skinless chicken breasts, pounded
- **2** plum tomatoes, diced
- **2** red peppers, chopped
- **1 1/2 cups** marinara sauce
- **1 cup** fat-free shredded mozzarella cheese
- **2 tablespoons** chopped fresh basil
- **1 1/2 tablespoons** chopped fresh oregano
- salt and pepper to taste

1. Preheat the oven to 375°F.

2. Season the chicken with salt and pepper.

3. Cook tomatoes, peppers and herbs until hot. Remove from heat and stir in half the cheese. Season with salt and pepper.

4. Divide the mixture onto each chicken breast. Roll up and put in a baking dish.

5. Spread the marinara sauce on the chicken then top with the remaining cheese. Bake for 45 minutes.

| CALORIES | CARBS | SUGAR | FAT | PROTEIN | SODIUM |
|----------|-------|-------|-----|---------|--------|
| 104 | 5.5 | 1.7 | 1.0 | 16.9 | 327 |
| KCAL | GRAMS | GRAMS | GRAMS | GRAMS | MILLIGRAMS |

# WHITE BEAN AND CHICKEN CHILI

**SERVES**
**8**

**PREP TIME**
**40**
MINUTES

**COOK TIME**
**25**
MINUTES

**1.** Season the chicken with salt and pepper. Spray a large skillet. Brown the chicken. Set aside.

**2.** Sauté onion until fragrant. Add garlic, chili, cumin, coriander and chili powder. Cook for 1 minute. Add chicken and broth back to the pot. Cover and simmer for 30 minutes.

**3.** Remove the chicken and add the white beans. Shred the chicken and return to the pot. Simmer for 5-10 minutes until the sauce reduces to desired consistency.

- **1 pound** chicken tender
- **1** 15.5-ounce **can** white beans, rinsed and drained
- **2 ounces** diced green chilies
- **1 cup** chopped onion
- **1** poblano chili, seeded and chopped
- **2 cloves** garlic, minced
- **2 cups** low sodium chicken broth
- **1 teaspoon** chili powder
- **1 teaspoon** ground cumin
- **1 teaspoon** ground coriander
- salt and pepper to taste

| CALORIES | CARBS | SUGAR | FAT | PROTEIN | SODIUM |
|---|---|---|---|---|---|
| 115 | 12.0 | 1.7 | 0.6 | 15.2 | 322 |
| KCAL | GRAMS | GRAMS | GRAMS | GRAMS | MILLIGRAMS |

# NORTHERN ITALIAN CHICKEN STEW

 **SERVES**
8

 **PREP TIME**
10
MINUTES

 **COOK TIME**
60
MINUTES

- **1 pound** chicken tender

- **1/2 cup** chopped onion

- **1/2 cup** sliced carrot

- **1/2 cup** sliced red bell pepper

- **1 cup** crushed tomatoes

- **2 cloves** garlic, minced

- **1** bay leave

- **2 tablespoons** dry white wine

- **1 tablespoon** chopped fresh parsley

- **1 teaspoon** minced rosemary

1. Season the chicken with salt and pepper. Spray a large skillet. Brown the chicken. Set aside.

2. Sauté the onion, carrot, bell peppers, garlic, bay leave and rosemary until fragrant. Add wine, tomato and chicken. Bring to a boil then reduce to low. Cover and simmer for 30 minutes.

| CALORIES | CARBS | SUGAR | FAT | PROTEIN | SODIUM |
|----------|-------|-------|-----|---------|--------|
| 77 | 4.8 | 2.4 | 0.3 | 11.9 | 145 |
| KCAL | GRAMS | GRAMS | GRAMS | GRAMS | MILLIGRAMS |

# MUSTARD AND WINE BRAISED CHICKEN

 **SERVES**
8

 **PREP TIME**
10
MINUTES

 **COOK TIME**
60
MINUTES

**1.** Preheat the oven to 375°F.

**2.** Season the chicken with salt and pepper. Spray a large skillet. Brown the chicken. Set aside.

**3.** Sauté onion, garlic and shallots until fragrant. Add chicken, wine, mustard and broth back to the pot. Cover and bake for 45 minutes.

- **1 pound** chicken tender

- 2 shallots, chopped

- **2 cloves** garlic, minced

- **3/4 cup** low sodium chicken broth

- **1/2 cup** dry white wine

- **2 tablespoons** mustard

- **1 tablespoon** chopped fresh thyme

- salt and pepper to taste

| CALORIES | CARBS | SUGAR | FAT | PROTEIN | SODIUM |
|----------|-------|-------|-----|---------|--------|
| 71 | 1.6 | 0.6 | 0.3 | 11.4 | 105 |
| KCAL | GRAMS | GRAMS | GRAMS | GRAMS | MILLIGRAMS |

# YAKITORI CHICKEN

 **SERVES**
8

 **PREP TIME**
8
HOURS

 **COOK TIME**
10
MINUTES

- **1 pound** chicken tender

- 2 green onions, chopped

- **1/2 cup** fat-free low sodium chicken broth

- **1/4 cup** sherry cooking wine

- **3 tablespoons** low sodium soy sauce

- **1 tablespoon** grated ginger

- **2 cloves** garlic, minced

1. In a large resealable bag, add all ingredients. Seal and shake the bag to mix well. Marinate overnight.

2. Preheat the broiler. Thread the meat onto 16 skewers.

3. Broil 3-4 minutes on each side.

| CALORIES | CARBS | SUGAR | FAT | PROTEIN | SODIUM |
|----------|-------|-------|-----|---------|--------|
| 64 | 1.1 | 0.2 | 0.3 | 11.6 | 343 |
| KCAL | GRAMS | GRAMS | GRAMS | GRAMS | MILLIGRAMS |

# TUNA POKE

**1.** In a medium bowl, combine all ingredients and serve.

- **1/2 pound** sushi grade tuna, cubed
- **1/4 cup** finely chopped green onion
- **2 tablespoons** low sodium soy sauce
- **1 teaspoon** lime juice
- **1 teaspoon** roasted sesame seed

| CALORIES | CARBS | SUGAR | FAT | PROTEIN | SODIUM |
| --- | --- | --- | --- | --- | --- |
| 91 | 1.0 | 0.0 | 2.4 | 14.7 | 310 |
| KCAL | GRAMS | GRAMS | GRAMS | GRAMS | MILLIGRAMS |

# BROILED CURRY SALMON

 **SERVES** 4

 **PREP TIME** 10 MINUTES

 **COOK TIME** 10 MINUTES

- **2** salmon fillets ( 6-ounce each)

- **1 teaspoon** curry powder

- **1 teaspoon** garlic powder

- **1/2 teaspoon** cumin

- **1/4 teaspoon** salt

1. Preheat the broiler.

2. Mix the spice in a small bowl. Rub the spice evenly on the salmon.

3. Broil for 8-12 minutes.

| CALORIES | CARBS | SUGAR | FAT | PROTEIN | SODIUM |
|----------|-------|-------|-----|---------|--------|
| 80 | 0.9 | 0.0 | 0.9 | 18.2 | 256 |
| KCAL | GRAMS | GRAMS | GRAMS | GRAMS | MILLIGRAMS |

# PORTOBELLO TUNA MELT

 **SERVES**
4

 **PREP TIME**
5
MINUTES

 **COOK TIME**
20
MINUTES

1. Preheat the broiler

2. In a medium bowl, combine tuna, mayonnaise, sour cream, onion and season with salt and pepper

3. Divide the tuna mixture on the mushroom.

4. Place a slice of tomato on each mushroom. Then Top with mozzarella cheese.

5. Place the mushroom on a rack and broil for 10-15 minutes until the cheese turns golden brown.

- **4** Portobello Mushroom, Gills and stems removed

- **1** 5-ounce **can** tuna in water, drained

- **4 slices** tomatoes

- **1/4 cup** chopped onion

- **1/4 cup** low fat mayonnaise

- **1/4 cup** fat-free sour cream

- **1/4 cup** fat-free parmesan cheese

- **3/4 cup** fat-free mozzarella cheese

- salt and pepper to taste

| CALORIES | CARBS | SUGAR | FAT | PROTEIN | SODIUM |
|---|---|---|---|---|---|
| 137 | 14.8 | 3.7 | 1.8 | 17.5 | 620 |
| KCAL | GRAMS | GRAMS | GRAMS | GRAMS | MILLIGRAMS |

# BUFFALO RANCH SALMON

**SERVES**
**4**

**PREP TIME**
**10**
MINUTES

**COOK TIME**
**15**
MINUTES

- 2 salmon fillets ( 6-ounce each)

- **2 tablespoon** whole wheat breadcrumbs

- **2 tablespoons** buffalo sauce

- **1 tablespoons** fat-free ranch seasoning

- **1/4 teaspoon** salt

- **1/4 teaspoon** pepper

1. Preheat the oven to 425°F.

2. In a small bowl, combine buffalo sauce, ranch seasoning, salt and pepper.

3. Spread the sauce on each salmon fillets. Sprinkle the breadcrumbs on top of each fillet.

4. Bake for 15 minutes.

| CALORIES | CARBS | SUGAR | FAT | PROTEIN | SODIUM |
|----------|-------|-------|-----|---------|--------|
| 95 | 2.6 | 0.4 | 1.6 | 18.4 | 469 |
| KCAL | GRAMS | GRAMS | GRAMS | GRAMS | MILLIGRAMS |

# LEMON GLAZED SALMON

 **SERVES**
4

 **PREP TIME**
5
MINUTES

 **COOK TIME**
20
MINUTES

**1.** Brown the salmon fillet. Set aside.

**2.** Sauté garlic until fragrant.

**3.** Add lemon zest, lemon juice and broth. Simmer on low until reduces by half. Season with salt and pepper.

**4.** Return the Salmon. Simmer until the salmon is cooked through. Sprinkle parsley and serve.

- **2** salmon fillets ( 6-ounce each)

- **1** lemon, thinly sliced

- **2 tablespoons** lemon juice

- **1 tablespoon** lemon zest

- **3 cloves** garlic, minced

- **1 cup** fat-free low sodium chicken broth

- **2 tablespoons** chopped fresh parsley

- salt and pepper to taste

- Non-stick Cooking Spray

| CALORIES | CARBS | SUGAR | FAT | PROTEIN | SODIUM |
|----------|-------|-------|-----|---------|--------|
| 83 | 1.8 | 0.2 | 0.8 | 18.7 | 132 |
| KCAL | GRAMS | GRAMS | GRAMS | GRAMS | MILLIGRAMS |

# SMOKED SALMON SCRAMBLE

 SERVES
8

 PREP TIME
10
MINUTES

 COOK TIME
15
MINUTES

- **4 ounces** smoked salmon

- **2** large eggs and **4** egg whites

- **2 cups** baby spinach

- **2 cloves** garlic, minced

- **2 tablespoons** low fat cheddar cheese

- salt and pepper to taste

- Nonstick Cooking Spray

1. Sauté garlic and spinach until fragrant.

2. In a medium bowl, whisk the eggs and cheese. Season with salt and pepper.

3. Add the egg mixture. Scramble for 30 seconds.

4. Add salmon. Scramble for until eggs are cooked through.

| CALORIES | CARBS | SUGAR | FAT | PROTEIN | SODIUM |
|----------|-------|-------|-----|---------|--------|
| 97 | 1.4 | 0.4 | 3.9 | 13.1 | 320 |
| KCAL | GRAMS | GRAMS | GRAMS | GRAMS | MILLIGRAMS |

# TILAPIA TOMATO ALFREDO

 **SERVES**
8

 **PREP TIME**
5
MINUTES

 **COOK TIME**
20
MINUTES

**1.** Season the fish with salt and pepper. Set aside.

**2.** Sauté garlic and onion until fragrant.

**3.** Add soup, milk and tomatoes. Cook until bubbly. Add Fish and bring it to a boil. Then reduce to low and simmer for 10-15 minutes.

- **1 pound** tilapia fillet, cut into 2-inch pieces

- 1 10.5-ounce **can** fat-free condensed cream of mushroom soup

- 1 10-ounce **can** diced tomatoes, drained

- **1/2 cup** chopped onion

- **3 cloves** garlic, minced

- **1/2 cup** skim milk

- **2 tablespoons** chopped fresh parsley

- salt and pepper to taste

- Nonstick Cooking Spray

| CALORIES | CARBS | SUGAR | FAT | PROTEIN | SODIUM |
|----------|-------|-------|-----|---------|--------|
| 84 | 5.8 | 1.8 | 2.1 | 11.3 | 324 |
| KCAL | GRAMS | GRAMS | GRAMS | GRAMS | MILLIGRAMS |

# SPICY HALIBUT PARMESAN

 **SERVES**
8

 **PREP TIME**
15
MINUTES

 **COOK TIME**
10
MINUTES

- **1 pound** skinless halibut fillets

- **1** green onion, chopped

- **1/2 cup** fat-free parmesan cheese

- **1 1/2 tablespoons** fat-free mayonnaise

- **1 tablespoons** lemon juice

- **1 teaspoon** hot sauce

- **1/4 teaspoon** salt

- Nonstick Cooking Spray

1. Preheat the oven to 425°F.

2. In a medium bowl, combine all ingredients except fish.

3. Season the fish with salt and pepper. Place the fish on a baking dish. Bake for 10 minutes.

4. Spread the cheese mixture on top and bake for another 5 minutes or until cheese are bubbly and golden brown.

| CALORIES | CARBS | SUGAR | FAT | PROTEIN | SODIUM |
|----------|-------|-------|-----|---------|--------|
| 68 | 3.8 | 0.3 | 0.5 | 12.5 | 270 |
| KCAL | GRAMS | GRAMS | GRAMS | GRAMS | MILLIGRAMS |

# ASIAN SALMON MEATBALLS

 **SERVES**
6

 **PREP TIME**
5
MINUTES

 **COOK TIME**
25
MINUTES

**1.** Preheat the oven to 350°F.

**2.** In a large bowl, combine all ingredients. Divide the mixture into 12 meatballs. Apply nonstick cooking spray.

**3.** Bake for 15-18 minutes.

- **12 ounces** canned pink salmon, drained
- **1/2 cup** whole wheat breadcrumbs
- **2** green onions, finely chopped
- **2 cloves** garlic, minced
- **1/2 tablespoon** grated ginger
- **1** egg
- **1/4 teaspoon** salt
- **1/4 teaspoon** ground black pepper

| CALORIES | CARBS | SUGAR | FAT | PROTEIN | SODIUM |
|---|---|---|---|---|---|
| 99 | 5.6 | 0.5 | 2.5 | 14.2 | 296 |
| KCAL | GRAMS | GRAMS | GRAMS | GRAMS | MILLIGRAMS |

# SPICY PEANUT SALMON BURGER

SERVES
6

PREP TIME
5
MINUTES

COOK TIME
25
MINUTES

- **12 ounces** canned pink salmon, drained

- **1/2 cup** whole wheat breadcrumbs

- **2** green onions, finely chopped

- **1 1/2 tablespoons** low sodium soy sauce

- **2 tablespoons** powdered peanut butter

- **1 tablespoon** hot sauce

- **1/4 cup** fat-free Greek yogurt

**1.** Preheat the oven to 350°F.

**2.** In a large bowl, combine all ingredients. Divide the mixture into 12 patties. Apply nonstick cooking spray.

**3.** Bake for 15-18 minutes.

| CALORIES | CARBS | SUGAR | FAT | PROTEIN | SODIUM |
|---|---|---|---|---|---|
| 120 | 7.0 | 0.9 | 3.4 | 16.1 | 477 |
| KCAL | GRAMS | GRAMS | GRAMS | GRAMS | MILLIGRAMS |

# ASIAN GINGER CATFISH

 **SERVES**
**8**

 **PREP TIME**
**15**
MINUTES

 **COOK TIME**
**20**
MINUTES

**1.** Sauté ginger until golden brown. Sear the fish. 3 minutes on each side. Set aside.

**2.** Sauté garlic, green onion, onion and bell peppers until fragrant. Add fish sauce, soy sauce and oyster sauce. Return the fish and bury the fish in the sauce and cook for 3-5 more minutes.

- **1 pound** catfish fillet, cut into 2-inch pieces

- **4 ounces** fresh ginger, peeled and cut into thin strips

- **1/2 cup** chopped onion

- **1/2 cup** sliced red bell peppers

- **2** green onions, chopped

- **2 tablespoons** fish sauce

- **1 tablespoons** oyster sauce

- **1 tablespoon** low-sodium soy sauce

- Nonstick Cooking Spray

| CALORIES | CARBS | SUGAR | FAT | PROTEIN | SODIUM |
|----------|-------|-------|-----|---------|--------|
| 123 | 3.5 | 1.2 | 1.0 | 12.3 | 518 |
| KCAL | GRAMS | GRAMS | GRAMS | GRAMS | MILLIGRAMS |

# CHEESY TUNA CASSEROLE

 SERVES
**8**

 PREP TIME
**10**
MINUTES

 COOK TIME
**30**
MINUTES

- **3** 5-ounce **cans** tuna in water, drained
- **1** medium head cauliflower, cut into florets
- **1 cup** diced onion
- **1 cup** low-fat alfredo sauce
- **1 cup** skim milk
- **1/2 cup** fat-free parmesan cheese
- **1 cup** fat-free mozzarella cheese
- Nonstick Cooking Spray

**1.** Preheat the broiler

**2.** In a large pot, add enough water to cover the cauliflower. Cook until cauliflower is soft. Drain and mash the cauliflower. Season with salt and pepper.

**3.** Sauté onion until fragrant. Add milk and alfredo sauce. Stir in the parmesan cheese, tuna and cauliflower mash. Adjust seasoning if needed.

**4.** Top with mozzarella cheese and broil until the cheese is golden brown and bubbly.

| CALORIES | CARBS | SUGAR | FAT | PROTEIN | SODIUM |
|---|---|---|---|---|---|
| 148 | 12.0 | 4.2 | 3.5 | 18.0 | 670 |
| KCAL | GRAMS | GRAMS | GRAMS | GRAMS | MILLIGRAMS |

# MEDITERRANEAN WHITE FISH

 **SERVES**
8

 **PREP TIME**
15
MINUTES

 **COOK TIME**
30
MINUTES

1. Preheat the oven to 425°F.

2. Season the fish with salt and pepper. Place the fish on a baking dish. Set aside.

3. Sauté garlic and onion until fragrant. Then add tomatoes and cook until tender. Add capers, olives, wine, oregano and basil. Reduce to low heat. Stir in cheese. Cook on low until the sauce reduces by half.

4. Spread the sauce on the fish. Bake for 10-15 minutes.

- **1 pound** white fish fillet
- **5** plum tomatoes, diced
- **1/2 cup** chopped onion
- **2 cloves** garlic, minced
- **4 tablespoons** capers
- **6** black olives, pitted and chopped
- **1/4 cup** dry white wine
- **3 tablespoons** fat-free parmesan cheese
- **1/2 teaspoon** dried basil
- pinch of dried oregano

| CALORIES | CARBS | SUGAR | FAT | PROTEIN | SODIUM |
|---|---|---|---|---|---|
| 98 | 3.8 | 1.8 | 1.3 | 14.8 | 340 |
| KCAL | GRAMS | GRAMS | GRAMS | GRAMS | MILLIGRAMS |

# GARLIC HERB TUNA STEAK

SERVES
**4**

PREP TIME
**40**
MINUTES

COOK TIME
**10**
MINUTES

- 2 tuna steak (6-ounce each)
- **2 cloves** garlic, minced
- **2 tablespoons** lemon juice
- **2 teaspoons** minced fresh thyme
- **1/4 teaspoon** salt
- **1/4 teaspoon** pepper

**1.** In a large resealable plastic bag, combine all ingredients. Put in the refrigerator and marinade for 30 minutes.

**2.** Preheat the broiler.

**3.** Discard the marinade, broil the tuna steak 3-4 minutes on each side.

| CALORIES | CARBS | SUGAR | FAT | PROTEIN | SODIUM |
|----------|-------|-------|-----|---------|--------|
| 95 | 1.3 | 0.2 | 0.8 | 19.7 | 173 |
| KCAL | GRAMS | GRAMS | GRAMS | GRAMS | MILLIGRAMS |

# SPICY HUMMUS TUNA CAKE

 **SERVES**
**12**

 **PREP TIME**
**20**
MINUTES

 **COOK TIME**
**40**
MINUTES

**1.** Preheat the oven to 350°F.

**2.** In a large bowl, combine all ingredients.

**3.** Spray a muffin tin. Divide the mixture into 12 cups.

**4.** Bake for 40 minutes.

- **3** 5-ounce **cans** tuna in water, drained

- **1 cup** roasted red pepper hummus

- **2 cloves** garlic, minced

- **1** green onion, chopped

- **1** jalapeno pepper, seeded and chopped

- **2** large eggs

- **1/4 teaspoon** salt

| CALORIES | CARBS | SUGAR | FAT | PROTEIN | SODIUM |
|----------|-------|-------|-----|---------|--------|
| 85 | 4.3 | 0.1 | 3.8 | 8.7 | 312 |
| KCAL | GRAMS | GRAMS | GRAMS | GRAMS | MILLIGRAMS |

# BALSAMIC PORK TENDERLOIN

**SERVES**
**6**

**PREP TIME**
**15**
MINUTES

**COOK TIME**
**10**
MINUTES

- **1 pound** pork tenderloin, cut into 1.5-inch piece

- **1/4 cup** fat-free low sodium chicken broth

- **2 tablespoons** balsamic vinegar

- **2 tablespoons** whole wheat flour

- **1 teaspoon** capers

- **1 teaspoon** lemon zest

- **1/2 teaspoon** salt

- **1/4 teaspoon** pepper

**1.** In a small bowl, mix together flour, salt and pepper. Coat the pork in the mixture. Shake off excess flour.

**2.** Brown the pork. Add vinegar and broth. Bring to a boil and reduce to low. Simmer for 4-5 minutes until pork is cooked through.

**3.** Remove the pork. Add lemon zest and capers. Simmer until the desired consistency. Pour the sauce over the pork and serve.

| CALORIES | CARBS | SUGAR | FAT | PROTEIN | SODIUM |
|---|---|---|---|---|---|
| 77 | 2.7 | 0.8 | 1.4 | 15.0 | 550 |
| KCAL | GRAMS | GRAMS | GRAMS | GRAMS | MILLIGRAMS |

# PORK AND BROCCOLI STIR FRY

 **SERVES**
**8**

 **PREP TIME**
**5**
MINUTES

 **COOK TIME**
**20**
MINUTES

1. In a large bowl, mix the pork with soy sauce, garlic, ground ginger and crushed red pepper. Set aside to marinate.

2. Blanch the broccoli in a pot of boiling water until slightly softened. Drain and set aside.

3. Sauté onion until fragrant. Set aside.

4. Add the pork without the marinate. Cook until cook through.

5. Dissolve the flour in the broth. Add broth and sauce. Cook until sauce thickens.

6. Add the broccoli and onion. Stir fry for 2-3 minutes until cooked through.

- **1 pound** pork tenderloin, thinly sliced
- **12 ounces** broccoli floret
- **1 cup** sliced onion
- **2 cloves** garlic, minced
- **1 cup** fat free low sodium chicken broth
- **2 tablespoons** low sodium soy sauce
- **1 tablespoon** whole wheat flour
- **1/4 teaspoon** ground ginger
- **1/8 teaspoon** crushed red pepper
- Nonstick Cooking Spray

| CALORIES | CARBS | SUGAR | FAT | PROTEIN | SODIUM |
|---|---|---|---|---|---|
| 78 | 6.0 | 1.3 | 1.2 | 13.0 | 364 |
| KCAL | GRAMS | GRAMS | GRAMS | GRAMS | MILLIGRAMS |

# PORK CHOPS IN MUSHROOM SAUCE

 **SERVES**
**8**

 **PREP TIME**
**10**
MINUTES

 **COOK TIME**
**40**
MINUTES

- **4** pork chops (4-ounce each)

- **1** 10.5-ounce **can** fat-free condensed cream of mushroom soup

- **2 cups** sliced mushrooms

- **1 cup** chopped onion

- **2 cloves** garlic, minced

- **2 tablespoons** dry white wine

- pinch of thyme

- salt and pepper to taste

- Nonstick Cooking Spray

1. Season the pork chops with salt and pepper.

2. Sauté garlic and onion until fragrant. Set aside.

3. Brown the pork chops. Add all ingredients and mix well. Cover and simmer on low for 20-25 minutes

| CALORIES | CARBS | SUGAR | FAT | PROTEIN | SODIUM |
|---|---|---|---|---|---|
| 107 | 6.0 | 0.9 | 3.1 | 13.1 | 521 |
| KCAL | GRAMS | GRAMS | GRAMS | GRAMS | MILLIGRAMS |

# PORK CHOPS IN CREAMY ONION SAUCE

 **SERVES**
**8**

 **PREP TIME**
**10**
MINUTES

 **COOK TIME**
**40**
MINUTES

**1.** Season the pork chops with salt and pepper.

**2.** Sauté garlic and onion until fragrant. Set aside.

**3.** Brown the pork chops. Add broth. Cover and simmer on low for 20-25 minutes.

**4.** Remove the pork chops. Simmer the sauce until reduces by half. Stir in sour cream and paprika. Pour the sauce over the pork chops and serve.

- **4** pork chops (4-ounce each)
- **1 1/2 cups** chopped onion
- **1/2 cup** fat-free low sodium chicken broth
- **1 clove** garlic, minced
- **3/4 cup** fat-free sour cream
- **2 teaspoons** paprika
- salt and pepper to taste
- Nonstick Cooking Spray

| CALORIES | CARBS | SUGAR | FAT | PROTEIN | SODIUM |
|----------|-------|-------|-----|---------|--------|
| 95 | 5.5 | 2.8 | 2.4 | 13.6 | 153 |
| KCAL | GRAMS | GRAMS | GRAMS | GRAMS | MILLIGRAMS |

# PORK STROGANOFF

**SERVES**
**8**

**PREP TIME**
**10**
MINUTES

**COOK TIME**
**40**
MINUTES

- **1 pound** pork tenderloin, cut into thin strips
- **2 cups** sliced mushrooms
- **1 cup** chopped onion
- **2 cloves** garlic, minced
- **1/2 cup** fat-free low-sodium chicken broth
- **1 cup** fat-free half and half
- **2 tablespoons** fat free sour cream
- **1 tablespoon** mustard
- **1 teaspoon** paprika
- **1 teaspoon** tomato paste
- **1 teaspoon** chili powder
- **1 teaspoon** lemon juice
- salt and pepper to taste

1. Season the pork chops with salt and pepper.

2. Sauté garlic, onion and mushrooms until fragrant. Set aside.

3. Brown the pork chops. Add broth. Cover and simmer on low for 20-25 minutes.

4. Remove the pork chops.

5. Stir in cream, mustard, tomato paste, lemon juice and other seasoning. Pour the sauce over the pork

| CALORIES | CARBS | SUGAR | FAT | PROTEIN | SODIUM |
|---|---|---|---|---|---|
| 93 | 7.3 | 2.7 | 1.5 | 13.6 | 448 |
| KCAL | GRAMS | GRAMS | GRAMS | GRAMS | MILLIGRAMS |

# VINEGAR MUSTARD GLAZED HAM LOAF

**SERVES**
**16**

**PREP TIME**
**10**
MINUTES

**COOK TIME**
**90**
MINUTES

**1.** Preheat the oven to 350°F.

**2.** In a large bowl, combine ham, pork, eggs, evaporated milk, salt and pepper. Spray a 9x13 baking dish. Place the mixture in the dish. Bake for 90 minutes.

**3.** In a small bowl, mix together vinegar, mustard and truvia. Pour the mixture on top of the loaf in the last 15 minutes.

- **2 pounds** extra lean ham

- **1 pound** extra lean ground pork

- **2** eggs

- **1 cup** whole wheat breadcrumbs

- **1 cup** low-fat evaporated milk

- **1/3 cup** Truvia brown sugar

- **1/4 cup** apple cider vinegar

- **1 tablespoon** mustard powder

- **1/4 teaspoon** salt

- **1/4 teaspoon** ground black pepper

| CALORIES | CARBS | SUGAR | FAT | PROTEIN | SODIUM |
|---|---|---|---|---|---|
| 146 | 9.6 | 4.3 | 4.7 | 17.3 | 755 |
| KCAL | GRAMS | GRAMS | GRAMS | GRAMS | MILLIGRAMS |

# GARLIC LEMON SCALLOPS

 **SERVES**
8

 **PREP TIME**
5
MINUTES

 **COOK TIME**
10
MINUTES

- **1 pound** sea scallops, patted dry

- **6 cloves** garlic, minced

- **2 scallions**, finely chopped

- **1 lemon**, juice only

- **1 tablespoon** whole wheat flour

- **1/4 teaspoon** salt

- pinch of ground sage

- Nonstick cooking spray

**1.** In a bowl, mix scallops with flour and salt.

**2.** Spray a large skillet, Sear the scallops until golden brown. Set aside.

**3.** sauté garlic and scallion until fragrant. Add lemon juice and return scallops. Stir well and cook for 30 seconds. Sprinkle with parsley and serve.

| CALORIES | CARBS | SUGAR | FAT | PROTEIN | SODIUM |
|---|---|---|---|---|---|
| 72 | 5.2 | 0.2 | 0.5 | 11.7 | 450 |
| KCAL | GRAMS | GRAMS | GRAMS | GRAMS | MILLIGRAMS |

# SCALLOPS IN JALAPENO WHISKY CREAM SAUCE

 **SERVES** 8

 **PREP TIME** 5 MINUTES

 **COOK TIME** 10 MINUTES

1. In a bowl, mix scallops with flour and 1/4 teaspoon salt. Spray a large skillet, Sear the scallops until golden brown. Set aside.

2. sauté garlic and pepper until fragrant. Add whisky and cook for 1 minute. Stir in cream and bring to a simmer. Season with salt and pepper.

3. Pour sauce over scallops. Sprinkle with chopped cilantro and serve.

- **1 pound** sea scallops, patted dry
- **2 cloves** garlic, minced
- **2** jalapeno pepper, seeded and finely chopped
- **1 cup** fat-free half and half
- **1/2 cup** chopped fresh cilantro
- **1/8 cup** bourbon whiskey
- **1 tablespoon** whole wheat flour
- **3/4 teaspoon** salt
- **1/2 teaspoon** ground black pepper

| CALORIES | CARBS | SUGAR | FAT | PROTEIN | SODIUM |
|----------|-------|-------|-----|---------|--------|
| 96 | 7.1 | 1.7 | 0.9 | 12.4 | 623 |
| KCAL | GRAMS | GRAMS | GRAMS | GRAMS | MILLIGRAMS |

# LOWCOUNTRY SHRIMPS

 **SERVES**
8

 **PREP TIME**
5
MINUTES

 **COOK TIME**
15
MINUTES

- **1 pound** fresh shrimps, peeled and deveined

- **1** 6.5-ounce **link** lean turkey sausage, sliced

- **1 cup** sliced bell pepper

- **2 cloves** garlic, minced

- **1 teaspoon** old bay seasoning

- **1/4 teaspoon** ground black pepper

- **1/4 cup** water

- Nonstick Cooking Spray

1. In a large bowl, season shrimp with old bay seasoning and black pepper. Set aside.

2. Spray a large skillet, sauté garlic until fragrant. Add sausage and cook until crispy. Add shrimp and water. Cook while stirring until cook through.

| CALORIES | CARBS | SUGAR | FAT | PROTEIN | SODIUM |
|----------|-------|-------|-----|---------|--------|
| 75 | 1.2 | 0.4 | 1.6 | 13.5 | 448 |
| KCAL | GRAMS | GRAMS | GRAMS | GRAMS | MILLIGRAMS |

# CHEESY ONION SCALLOPS

 **SERVES**
**8**

 **PREP TIME**
**5**
MINUTES

 **COOK TIME**
**15**
MINUTES

1. Preheat the broiler.

2. In a bowl, mix scallops with flour and 1/4 teaspoon salt. Spray an oven-proof skillet. Sear the scallops until golden brown. Set aside.

3. sauté garlic, onion and shallots until fragrant. Add wine and water. Simmer until the sauce reduces by half. Season with salt and pepper.

4. Stir in the scallops. Top with cheese and broil for 3-5 minutes until cheese turns golden brown.

- **1 pound** sea scallops, patted dry
- **2 cloves** garlic, minced
- 2 shallots, chopped
- **1/4 cup** chopped onion
- **3/4 cup** white wine
- **1/4 cup** water
- **1/4 cup** fat-free parmesan cheese
- **1** bay leave
- **2 tablespoons** chopped fresh thyme
- **1 tablespoon** whole wheat flour
- salt and pepper to taste

| CALORIES | CARBS | SUGAR | FAT | PROTEIN | SODIUM |
|----------|-------|-------|-----|---------|--------|
| 94 | 6.0 | 0.3 | 0.5 | 12.1 | 460 |
| KCAL | GRAMS | GRAMS | GRAMS | GRAMS | MILLIGRAMS |

# SHRIMP À LA GRECQUE

 **SERVES** 8

 **PREP TIME** 5 MINUTES

 **COOK TIME** 20 MINUTES

- **1 pound** fresh shrimps, peeled and deveined

- **1 1/2 cups** canned crushed tomatoes, drained

- **3 ounces** fat-free feta cheese, cubed

- **2 cloves** garlic, minced

- **1/2 cup** dry white wine

- **2 tablespoons** chopped fresh parsley

- **1/2 teaspoon** dried oregano, crushed

- **1/4 teaspoon** salt

- **1/4 teaspoon** ground black pepper

1. Spray a large skillet, sauté garlic until fragrant. Add tomatoes, wine, oregano, salt and pepper. Cook until sauce thickens.

2. Add shrimp, cook while stirring until cook through. Remove from heat. Add cheese and parsley before serving.

| CALORIES | CARBS | SUGAR | FAT | PROTEIN | SODIUM |
|----------|-------|-------|-----|---------|--------|
| 97 | 4.3 | 1.7 | 0.9 | 14.1 | 507 |
| KCAL | GRAMS | GRAMS | GRAMS | GRAMS | MILLIGRAMS |

# CRAB IMPERIAL

 **SERVES**
**8**

 **PREP TIME**
**10**
MINUTES

 **COOK TIME**
**20**
MINUTES

1. Preheat the oven to 400°F.

2. In a large bowl, combine all

3. ingredients except paprika and cilantro.

4. Transfer the mixture to a baking dish. Sprinkle Paprika and bake for 20 minutes. Garnish with fresh cilantro and serve.

- **1 pound** crab meat
- **1/2 cup** chopped bell peppers
- **1/2 cup** chopped celery
- **2 egg whites**, beaten
- **1/2** lemon, juice only
- **1 cup** fat-free plain yogurt
- **2 tablespoons** chopped fresh cilantro
- **1 teaspoon** dry mustard
- **1/4 teaspoon** salt
- **1/4 teaspoon** Worcestershire sauce
- **1/8 teaspoon** chili powder
- **1/8 teaspoon** paprika

| CALORIES | CARBS | SUGAR | FAT | PROTEIN | SODIUM |
|---|---|---|---|---|---|
| 76 | 10.8 | 4.9 | 0.6 | 7.4 | 423 |
| KCAL | GRAMS | GRAMS | GRAMS | GRAMS | MILLIGRAMS |

# STEAMED CLAMS IN GARLIC WINE SAUCE

 **SERVES** 5

 **PREP TIME** 10 MINUTES

 **COOK TIME** 25 MINUTES

- **50** small clams, scrubbed
- **1 cup** white wine
- **8 cloves** garlic, minced
- **1/2 cup** chopped fresh parsley
- **1 tablespoon** butter
- salt and pepper to taste
- Nonstick Cooking Spray

1. Spray a large skillet, sauté garlic until fragrant. Add wine. Simmer until sauce reduces by half, about 15 minutes.

2. Add clams, cover and steam until clams begin to open, about 5 minutes.

3. Stir in butter and cover. Steam until most clams open, about 5 minutes. Season with salt and pepper. Sprinkle with parsley and serve.

| CALORIES | CARBS | SUGAR | FAT | PROTEIN | SODIUM |
|----------|-------|-------|-----|---------|--------|
| 168 | 5.7 | 0.1 | 3.6 | 18.9 | 111 |
| KCAL | GRAMS | GRAMS | GRAMS | GRAMS | MILLIGRAMS |

# MUSSELS IN MARINARA SAUCE

 **SERVES**
**6**

 **PREP TIME**
**10**
MINUTES

 **COOK TIME**
**30**
MINUTES

**1.** Spray a large skillet, sauté garlic until fragrant. Add wine. Simmer until sauce reduces by half, about 15 minutes.

**2.** Add tomatoes and green onion and cook for 4-5 minutes until softens.

**3.** Add mussels. Cover and cook until mussels start to open, about 5 minutes. Stir in butter. cover and cook until most mussels open.

**4.** Sprinkle with parsley and serve.

- **50** mussels, scrubbed and debearded

- **6 cloves** garlic, minced

- **3** plum tomatoes, chopped

- **3** green onion, chopped

- **1/2 cup** chopped fresh parsley

- **1 cup** white wine

- **1 tablespoon** butter

- salt and pepper to taste

- Nonstick Cooking Spray

| CALORIES | CARBS | SUGAR | FAT | PROTEIN | SODIUM |
|----------|-------|-------|-----|---------|--------|
| 174 | 8.1 | 1.3 | 4.9 | 16.9 | 410 |
| KCAL | GRAMS | GRAMS | GRAMS | GRAMS | MILLIGRAMS |

# CREAMY CAJUN SHRIMPS

**SERVES**
**12**

**PREP TIME**
**10**
MINUTES

**COOK TIME**
**30**
MINUTES

- **1 1/2 pounds** fresh shrimps, peeled and deveined

- **1/2 cup** sliced mushrooms

- **2** green onions, chopped

- **1/4 cup** low-fat alfredo sauce

- **1/4 cup** chopped fresh parsley

- **1/4 cup** skim milk

- **1/4 cup** fat-free grated parmesan cheese

- **1 tablespoon** Cajun seasoning

- salt and pepper to taste

- Nonstick Cooking Spray

1. Preheat the oven to 350°F.

2. Season the shrimp with Cajun seasoning, salt and pepper.

3. Spray a large skillet, sauté mushrooms and green onion until fragrant. Add shrimp and sauté until cooked through. Transfer to a baking Dish.

4. Add alfredo sauce and skim milk to the pan and stir to combine.

   Pour the sauce over the shrimps. Sprinkle with parmesan cheese and bake for 20 minutes.

| CALORIES | CARBS | SUGAR | FAT | PROTEIN | SODIUM |
|----------|-------|-------|-----|---------|--------|
| 69 | 1.2 | 0.4 | 1.3 | 12.7 | 485 |
| KCAL | GRAMS | GRAMS | GRAMS | GRAMS | MILLIGRAMS |

# MARYLAND CRAB CAKE

 **SERVES**
8

 **PREP TIME**
60
MINUTES

 **COOK TIME**
15
MINUTES

**1.** In a large bowl, combine crabmeat, egg, half of the breadcrumbs, mayonnaise, mustard, Worcestershire sauce and all seasoning. Refrigerate for 1 hour.

**2.** Spread the remaining breadcrumbs on a large plate.

**3.** Divide the crab mixture into 8 portions and shape into patties. Coat with bread crumbs on each side.

**4.** Spray a pan, cook the crab cakes until golden brown on each side.

- **1 pound** crab meat
- **1/2 cup** whole wheat breadcrumbs, divided
- **2 tablespoons** fat-free mayonnaise
- **1 egg**, beaten
- **1/2 teaspoon** Dijon Mustard
- **1/2 teaspoon** Old Bay seasoning
- **1/4 teaspoon** Worcestershire sauce
- **1/4 teaspoon** salt
- **1/8 teaspoon** ground black pepper
- Nonstick cooking spray

| CALORIES | CARBS | SUGAR | FAT | PROTEIN | SODIUM |
|----------|-------|-------|-----|---------|--------|
| 69 | 4.1 | 0.6 | 0.7 | 11.5 | 346 |
| KCAL | GRAMS | GRAMS | GRAMS | GRAMS | MILLIGRAMS |

# GRILLED TOMATO BASIL SHRIMPS

SERVES
**8**

PREP TIME
**2**
HOURS

COOK TIME
**15**
MINUTES

- **1 pound** fresh shrimps, peeled and deveined

- **4 cloves** garlic, minced

- **3 tablespoons** tomato sauce

- **2 tablespoons** chopped fresh basil

- **1 tablespoons** red wine vinegar

- **1 tablespoon** olive oil

- **1/4 teaspoon** salt

- **1/8 teaspoon** cayenne pepper

- Nonstick Cooking Spray

**1.** In a large resealable bag, add all ingredients and mix well. Seal the bag and refrigerate for 2 hours to marinate.

**2.** Prepare the grill. Thread the shrimp onto skewers. Spray the Grill. Cook shrimp for 2-3 minutes on each side or until opaque

| CALORIES | CARBS | SUGAR | FAT | PROTEIN | SODIUM |
|----------|-------|-------|-----|---------|--------|
| 77 | 0.9 | 0.5 | 2.6 | 12.2 | 361 |
| KCAL | GRAMS | GRAMS | GRAMS | GRAMS | MILLIGRAMS |

# GRILLED LEMON GINGER SHRIMPS

 **SERVES**
8

 **PREP TIME**
10
MINUTES

 **COOK TIME**
50
MINUTES

1. In a large resealable bag, add all ingredients and mix well. Seal the bag and refrigerate for 2 hours to marinate.

2. Prepare the grill. Thread the shrimp onto skewers. Spray the Grill. Cook shrimp for 2-3 minutes on each side or until opaque

- **1 pound** fresh shrimps, peeled and deveined

- **4 cloves** garlic, minced

- **1/4 cup** lemon juice

- **1/4 cup** chopped fresh cilantro

- **3 tablespoons** grated ginger

- **1 teaspoon** paprika

- **1/4 teaspoon** salt

- **1/4 teaspoon** ground black pepper

| CALORIES | CARBS | SUGAR | FAT | PROTEIN | SODIUM |
|---|---|---|---|---|---|
| 66 | 1.9 | 0.3 | 1.0 | 12.4 | 345 |
| KCAL | GRAMS | GRAMS | GRAMS | GRAMS | MILLIGRAMS |

# TACO SALAD

- **1 pound** 97/3 lean ground beef

- **1 head** romaine lettuce, chopped

- **2** medium tomatoes, chopped

- **8** green onions, green and white separated and chopped

- **1 1/2 cups** fat-free shredded cheddar cheese

- **1/2 cup** fat-free Greek Yogurt

- **1/2 cup** salsa

- **1 tablespoon** chili powder

- salt and pepper to taste

1. Brown the beef with white part of onions. Season with chili powder, salt and pepper.

2. In a large bowl, toss all ingredients except yogurt and salsa together. Spoon yogurt and salsa on the side and serve.

| CALORIES | CARBS | SUGAR | FAT | PROTEIN | SODIUM |
|----------|-------|-------|-----|---------|--------|
| 134 | 7.6 | 2.7 | 2.4 | 21.8 | 376 |
| KCAL | GRAMS | GRAMS | GRAMS | GRAMS | MILLIGRAMS |

# ASIAN LETTUCE WRAP

SERVES
8

PREP TIME
15
MINUTES

COOK TIME
20
MINUTES

**1.** Spray a large skillet, sauté garlic, onion, green onion and water chestnut until fragrant. Drain the liquid and set aside.

**2.** Brown the beef. Then add all ingredients except lettuce. Stir well. Cook for another 2-3 minutes.

**3.** Divide the beef onto the lettuce leaves. Roll up and serve.

- **1 pound** 97/3 lean ground beef
- **1** 8-ounce **can** water chestnut, finely chopped
- **8** large romaine lettuce leaves
- **2 cloves** garlic, minced
- **1/2 cup** chopped onion
- **1/4 cup** chopped green onion
- **1/4 cup** hoisin sauce
- **2 tablespoons** low sodium soy sauce
- **2 tablespoon** rice wine vinegar
- **1 tablespoon** chili paste
- **1 tablespoon** grated ginger
- **1 tablespoon** sesame oil
- Nonstick cooking spray

| CALORIES | CARBS | SUGAR | FAT | PROTEIN | SODIUM |
|---|---|---|---|---|---|
| 121 | 9.0 | 3.5 | 4.1 | 13.0 | 351 |
| KCAL | GRAMS | GRAMS | GRAMS | GRAMS | MILLIGRAMS |

# SHRIMP SALAD STUFFED TOMATOES

 SERVES
8

 PREP TIME
35
MINUTES

 COOK TIME
/
MINUTES

- **1 pound** shrimp, peeled, deveined, cooked and chopped

- **4** large ripe tomatoes, cored

- **1 stalk** celery, chopped

- **1** shallot, minced

- **1/4 cup** chopped fresh basil

- **2 tablespoons** low-fat mayonnaise

- **1 tablespoon** white wine vinegar

- salt and pepper to taste

- pinch of paprika

**1.** In a medium bowl, combine shrimp, celery, shallots, basil, mayonnaise and vinegar. Season with salt and pepper.

**2.** Spoon the mixture into the tomatoes. Garnish with pinch of paprika and serve.

| CALORIES | CARBS | SUGAR | FAT | PROTEIN | SODIUM |
|----------|-------|-------|-----|---------|--------|
| 80 | 4.5 | 2.8 | 1.3 | 12.9 | 309 |
| KCAL | GRAMS | GRAMS | GRAMS | GRAMS | MILLIGRAMS |

# SLOPPY JOE LETTUCE WRAP

**SERVES**
8

**PREP TIME**
10
MINUTES

**COOK TIME**
40
MINUTES

1. Spray a large skillet, sauté garlic, onion and bell pepper until fragrant. Drain the liquid and set aside.

2. Brown the beef. Then add all ingredients except lettuce. Stir well. Reduce to low heat and simmer for 25 minutes.

3. Divide the beef onto the lettuce leaves. Roll up and serve.

- **1 pound** 97/3 lean ground beef

- **8 large** romaine lettuce leaves

- **3/4 cup** tomato sauce

- **1/4 cup** chopped onion

- **1/4 cup** chopped green bell peppers

- **2 cloves** garlic, minced.

- **1 teaspoon** yellow mustard

- **1 teaspoon** stevia

- salt and pepper to taste

- Nonstick Cooking Spray

| CALORIES | CARBS | SUGAR | FAT | PROTEIN | SODIUM |
|----------|-------|-------|-----|---------|--------|
| 82 | 3.6 | 1.6 | 2.2 | 12.8 | 155 |
| KCAL | GRAMS | GRAMS | GRAMS | GRAMS | MILLIGRAMS |

# GARDEN SALAD WITH LEMON CHICKEN AND FETA

 **SERVES**
**6**

 **PREP TIME**
**40**
MINUTES

 **COOK TIME**
**20**
MINUTES

## For Chicken:

- 2 boneless skinless chicken breasts
- 1/4 cup lemon juice
- 2 cloves garlic, minced
- 2 tablespoons chopped fresh dill
- 1/2 teaspoon salt
- 1/4 teaspoon ground black pepper
- Nonstick cooking spray

## For salad:

- 1/2 medium seedless cucumber, chopped
- 2 medium tomatoes, chopped
- 3 ounces fat-free feta cheese, cubed
- 2 tablespoons lemon juice
- 1 tablespoon olive oil
- 1/2 teaspoon Dijon mustard
- 1/2 teaspoon stevia
- salt and pepper to taste

**1.** In a medium resealable bag, add all ingredients for the chicken. Seal and press to coat the marinade evenly. Refrigerate for 30 minutes. Discard the marinade and dry the chicken.

**2.** Sear the chicken until golden brown on one side. Flip, reduce to low heat, cover and cook for 10-15 minutes until cooked through. Set aside to cool. Then slice into bite size.

**3.** Combine lemon juice, olive oil, mustard and stevia. In a large bowl, toss all ingredients together and serve.

| CALORIES | CARBS | SUGAR | FAT | PROTEIN | SODIUM |
|----------|-------|-------|-----|---------|--------|
| 111 | 8.5 | 3.1 | 2.9 | 12.9 | 475 |
| KCAL | GRAMS | GRAMS | GRAMS | GRAMS | MILLIGRAMS |

# BUFFALO CHICKEN LETTUCE WRAP

**SERVES**
**8**

**PREP TIME**
**10**
MINUTES

**COOK TIME**
**60**
MINUTES

1. Brown the chicken tender on both sides.

2. Add broth and beer. Cover and simmer for 1 hour.

3. Shredd the chicken. Add the chicken and buffalo sauce to a pan. Cook for 2-3 minutes. Season with salt.

4. Divide the chicken onto lettuce leaves. Top with cheese. Roll up and serve

- **1 pound** chicken tender

- **8** large romaine lettuce leave

- **1 cup** fat free low-sodium chicken broth

- **3/4 cup** beer

- **3 tablespoons** buffalo wing sauce

- **1/2 cup** low-fat crumbled blue cheese

- salt and pepper to taste

| CALORIES | CARBS | SUGAR | FAT | PROTEIN | SODIUM |
|---|---|---|---|---|---|
| 92 | 2.0 | 1.0 | 2.1 | 13.1 | 285 |
| KCAL | GRAMS | GRAMS | GRAMS | GRAMS | MILLIGRAMS |

# SEARED TANDOORI TOFU

**SERVES**
**5**

**PREP TIME**
**5**
MINUTES

**COOK TIME**
**10**
MINUTES

- 1 14-ounce **block** extra firm tofu, sliced into 1/2-inch slices
- **1 tablespoon** cayenne pepper
- **1 tablespoon** cumin
- **1 tablespoon** turmeric
- **1 tablespoon** smoked paprika
- **1/2 teaspoon** salt
- **1/2 teaspoon** black pepper
- Nonstick Cooking Spray

**1.** In a small bowl, mix all spices and seasoning together.

**2.** Spray a skillet. Heat on medium. Coat one side of the tofu and place the tofu face down. Sear both side until golden brown, around 2-3 minutes each side.

| CALORIES | CARBS | SUGAR | FAT | PROTEIN | SODIUM |
|---|---|---|---|---|---|
| 95 | 3.2 | 0.1 | 4.2 | 7.8 | 239 |
| KCAL | GRAMS | GRAMS | GRAMS | GRAMS | MILLIGRAMS |

# ITALIAN PORTOBELLO BAKE

**SERVES**
**12**

**PREP TIME**
**15**
MINUTES

**COOK TIME**
**15**
MINUTES

1. Preheat the oven to 400°F.

2. Spray a large skillet, sauté mushrooms until fragrant. Season with salt and pepper. Transfer to a baking dish.

3. In a medium bowl, Mix tomatoes with all herbs. Season with salt and pepper.

4. Spread the tomato mixture on the mushrooms. Top with cheese. Bake for 20-25 minutes.

- **1 pound** Portobello Mushroom, gill removed and thinly sliced

- **1** 14.5-ounce **can** crushed tomatoes

- **1 cup** fat-free parmesan cheese

- **1 cup** fat-free cheddar cheese

- **2 tablespoons** chopped fresh parsley

- **2 tablespoons** chopped fresh basil

- **1 teaspoon** dried oregano

- salt and pepper to taste

- Nonstick Cooking Spray

| CALORIES | CARBS | SUGAR | FAT | PROTEIN | SODIUM |
|---|---|---|---|---|---|
| 105 | 14.2 | 1.2 | 1.3 | 11.6 | 393 |
| KCAL | GRAMS | GRAMS | GRAMS | GRAMS | MILLIGRAMS |

# BAKED GARLIC TOFU

 **SERVES**
4

 **PREP TIME**
10
MINUTES

 **COOK TIME**
40
MINUTES

- 1 14-ounce **block** firm tofu, diced

- **4 cloves** garlic, minced

- **2 tablespoons** low-sodium soy sauce

- **1 tablespoon** cornstarch

- **2 teaspoons** stevia

- **1 teaspoon** sriracha sauce

- **1 teaspoon** onion powder

**1.** Preheat the oven to 400°F. Bake the tofu for 35-40 minutes until golden. Flipping once.

**2.** Spray a sauce pan, sauté garlic until fragrant. Add soy sauce, onion powder, stevia and sriracha sauce.

**3.** Dissolve the cornstarch in a few tablespoons of water. Slowly stir in the cornstarch mixture. Cook until sauce thickens.

| CALORIES | CARBS | SUGAR | FAT | PROTEIN | SODIUM |
|---|---|---|---|---|---|
| 102 | 6.6 | 0.3 | 4.7 | 8.9 | 325 |
| KCAL | GRAMS | GRAMS | GRAMS | GRAMS | MILLIGRAMS |

# Cooking Information Summary

**Method:** B-Baking     BR-Braising     G-Grilling     PF-Pan Fry     SF-Stir Fry

| Recipe Name | Time (min) | Method | No. of Ingredients | No. of condiments/ spice/herbs | Dairy Free? |
|---|---|---|---|---|---|
| Beef and Vegetables Stir Fry | 25 | SF | 6 | 4 | Yes |
| Thai Ground Beef | 30 | BR | 4 | 7 | Yes |
| Spicy Beef with Bok Choy | 35 | SF | 3 | 4 | Yes |
| Beef Stuffed Bell Pepper | 40 | B | 7 | 5 | |
| Salisbury Steak with Mushroom Sauce | 40 | BR | 8 | 0 | Yes |
| Mexican Beef Skillet | 45 | BR | 5 | 4 | Yes |
| Indian Beef Curry | 50 | BR | 6 | 5 | |
| Skinny Enchiladas | 55 | B | 6 | 2 | |
| Beef Chili | 70 | BR | 4 | 6 | Yes |
| Cheese-stuffed Meatloaf | 80 | B | 5 | 0 | |
| Italian Parmesan Meatballs | 90 | B | 4 | 3 | |
| Cabbage and Beef Bake | 95 | B | 9 | 0 | |
| Beer Braised Beef | 185 | BR | 3 | 3 | Yes |
| Sichuan Spicy Beef Stew | 135 | BR | 2 | 12 | Yes |
| Mongolian Beef Skewer | 490 | G | 1 | 6 | Yes |
| Chicken and Sugar Snap Pea Stir Fry | 25 | SF | 3 | 2 | Yes |
| lemon Thyme Chicken | 35 | BR | 3 | 2 | Yes |
| Pepper stuffed Cajun chicken | 35 | B | 4 | 1 | |

| Recipe Name | Time (min) | Method | No. of Ingredients | No. of condiments/ spice/herbs | Dairy Free? |
|---|---|---|---|---|---|
| Spinach Feta Chicken Roll | 35 | B | 5 | 3 | |
| Creamy Salsa Chicken | 40 | B | 3 | 1 | |
| Yogurt Chicken Parmesan | 55 | B | 3 | 1 | |
| Hungarian Chicken Paprikash | 60 | BR | 5 | 2 | |
| Rosemary Braised Chicken | 60 | B | 3 | 2 | Yes |
| Indonesian Coconut Chicken Opor | 65 | BR | 4 | 7 | Yes |
| Italian Stuffed Chicken Breast | 65 | B | 4 | 3 | |
| White Bean and Chicken Chili | 65 | BR | 4 | 6 | Yes |
| Northern Italian Chicken Stew | 70 | BR | 5 | 5 | Yes |
| Mustard and wine braised chicken | 70 | BR | 3 | 4 | Yes |
| Yakitori Chicken | 490 | G | 4 | 3 | Yes |
| Tuna Poke | 10 | / | 2 | 3 | Yes |
| Broiled Curry Salmon | 20 | G | 1 | 3 | Yes |
| Portobello Tuna Melt | 25 | B | 7 | 1 | |
| Buffalo Ranch Salmon | 25 | B | 2 | 2 | Yes |
| Lemon Glazed Salmon | 25 | BR | 5 | 2 | Yes |
| Smoked Salmon Scramble | 25 | SF | 4 | 1 | Yes |
| Tilapia Tomato Alfredo | 25 | BR | 5 | 2 | |
| Spicy Halibut Parmesan | 25 | B | 3 | 2 | |
| Asian Salmon Meatballs | 30 | B | 4 | 2 | Yes |
| Spicy Peanut Salmon Burger | 30 | B | 6 | 2 | |

| Recipe Name | Time (min) | Method | No. of Ingredients | No. of condiments/ spice/herbs | Dairy Free? |
|---|---|---|---|---|---|
| Asian Ginger catfish | 35 | BR | 4 | 4 | Yes |
| Cheesy Tuna Mini Casserole | 40 | B | 6 | 1 | |
| Mediterranean White Fish | 45 | BR | 5 | 5 | |
| Garlic Herb Tuna Steak | 50 | G | 2 | 2 | Yes |
| Spicy Tuna Cakes | 60 | B | 4 | 3 | Yes |
| Balsamic Pork tenderloin | 25 | BR | 5 | 1 | Yes |
| Pork and Broccoli Stir Fry | 25 | SF | 4 | 3 | Yes |
| Pork Chop in Mushroom Sauce | 50 | BR | 5 | 1 | |
| Pork Chop in Creamy Onion sauce | 50 | BR | 4 | 2 | |
| Pork Stroganoff | 50 | BR | 6 | 6 | |
| Vinegar Mustard Glazed Ham Loaf | 100 | B | 5 | 3 | |
| Garlic Lemon Scallops | 15 | BR | 4 | 2 | Yes |
| Scallops in Jalapeno Whisky Cream Sauce | 15 | BR | 4 | 3 | |
| Lowcountry Shrimps | 20 | BR | 3 | 2 | Yes |
| Cheesy Onion Scallops | 20 | BR | 5 | 3 | |
| Shrimp à la Grecque | 25 | BR | 4 | 3 | |
| Crab Imperial | 30 | B | 6 | 5 | |
| Steamed Clams in Garlic Wine Sauce | 35 | BR | 3 | 2 | |
| Mussels in Marinara Sauce | 40 | BR | 5 | 2 | |
| Creamy Cajun Shrimps | 40 | B | 5 | 3 | |
| Maryland Crab Cake | 75 | B | 3 | 4 | |

| Recipe Name | Time (min) | Method | No. of Ingredients | No. of condiments/ spice/herbs | Dairy Free? |
|---|---|---|---|---|---|
| Grilled Tomato Basil Marinated Shrimp | 135 | G | 2 | 5 | Yes |
| Grilled Lemon Ginger Shrimp | 135 | G | 2 | 4 | Yes |
| Taco Salad | 25 | SF | 6 | 2 | |
| Asian Lettuce Wrap | 35 | SF | 5 | 7 | Yes |
| Shrimp Salad Stuffed tomatoes | 35 | / | 4 | 3 | |
| Sloppy Joe Lettuce Wrap | 50 | BR | 5 | 3 | Yes |
| Garden Salad with lemon chicken and Feta | 60 | PF | 5 | 2 | |
| Buffalo Chicken Lettuce Wrap | 70 | BR | 5 | 1 | |
| Seared Tandoori Tofu | 15 | PF | 1 | 4 | Yes |
| Italian Portobello Bake | 30 | B | 3 | 3 | |
| Baked Garlic Tofu | 50 | B | 3 | 4 | Yes |

# Nutrition Information Summary

| Recipe Name | Calories (kCal) | Carbs (g) | Sugar (g) | Fat (g) | Protein (g) | Sodium (mg) |
|---|---|---|---|---|---|---|
| Beef and Vegetables Stir Fry | 99 | 4.6 | 1.9 | 2.6 | 13.4 | 337 |
| Thai Ground Beef | 106 | 4.1 | 2.1 | 3.9 | 13.0 | 270 |
| Spicy Beef with Bok Choy | 114 | 5.7 | 1.6 | 2.6 | 13.5 | 469 |
| Beef Stuffed Bell Pepper | 118 | 7.7 | 3.6 | 3.2 | 15.6 | 471 |
| Salisbury Steak with Mushroom Sauce | 120 | 5.0 | 0.9 | 2.9 | 17.0 | 566 |
| Mexican Beef Skillet | 102 | 4.4 | 1.9 | 2.7 | 13.2 | 339 |
| Indian Beef Curry | 113 | 6.4 | 2.9 | 3.3 | 15.0 | 316 |
| Skinny Enchiladas | 149 | 7.5 | 0.6 | 4.3 | 19.9 | 495 |
| Beef Chili | 147 | 14.6 | 3.7 | 3.3 | 15.7 | 227 |
| Cheese-stuffed Meatloaf | 83 | 3.6 | 0.5 | 1.6 | 13.7 | 412 |
| Italian Parmesan Meatballs | 116 | ·6.7 | 1.9 | 3.4 | 14.7 | 454 |
| Cabbage and Beef Bake | 131 | 9.0 | 4.8 | 3.1 | 17.6 | 313 |
| Beer Braised Beef | 96 | 3.6 | 0.8 | 2.0 | 13.0 | 247 |
| Sichuan Spicy Beef Stew | 84 | 2.4 | 0.7 | 2.0 | 13.0 | 102 |
| Mongolian Beef Skewer | 90 | 1.8 | 1.0 | 2.6 | 12.3 | 210 |
| Chicken and Sugar Snap Pea Stir Fry | 59 | 1.7 | 0.6 | 0.3 | 11.5 | 118 |
| Lemon Thyme Chicken | 55 | 1.0 | 0.2 | 0.2 | 11.3 | 56 |
| Pepper stuffed Cajun chicken | 91 | 4.0 | 1.6 | 0.6 | 16.3 | 522 |
| Spinach Feta Chicken Roll | 83 | 2.1 | 0.8 | 0.6 | 15.0 | 328 |
| Creamy Salsa Chicken | 92 | 5.5 | 4.0 | 0.2 | 12.0 | 296 |
| Yogurt Chicken Parmesan | 88 | 5.6 | 1.4 | 1.2 | 13.4 | 463 |

| Recipe Name | Calories (kCal) | Carbs (g) | Sugar (g) | Fat (g) | Protein (g) | Sodium (mg) |
|---|---|---|---|---|---|---|
| Hungarian Chicken Paprikash | 72 | 3.7 | 1.9 | 0.4 | 12.2 | 80 |
| Rosemary Braised Chicken | 81 | 1.2 | 0.5 | 0.3 | 11.0 | 57 |
| Indonesian Coconut Chicken Opor | 136 | 9.0 | 1.1 | 4.1 | 15.5 | 226 |
| Italian Stuffed Chicken Breast | 104 | 5.5 | 1.7 | 1.0 | 16.9 | 327 |
| White Bean and Chicken Chili | 115 | 12.0 | 1.7 | 0.6 | 15.2 | 322 |
| Northern Italian Chicken Stew | 77 | 4.8 | 2.4 | 0.3 | 11.9 | 145 |
| Mustard and wine braised chicken | 71 | 1.6 | 0.6 | 0.3 | 11.4 | 105 |
| Yakitori Chicken | 64 | 1.1 | 0.2 | 0.3 | 11.6 | 343 |
| Tuna Poke | 91 | 1.0 | 0.0 | 2.4 | 14.7 | 310 |
| Broiled Curry Salmon | 80 | 0.9 | 0.0 | 0.9 | 18.2 | 256 |
| Portobello Tuna Melt | 137 | 14.8 | 3.7 | 1.8 | 17.5 | 620 |
| Buffalo Ranch Salmon | 95 | 2.6 | 0.4 | 1.6 | 18.4 | 469 |
| Lemon Glazed Salmon | 83 | 1.8 | 0.2 | 0.8 | 18.7 | 132 |
| Smoked Salmon Scramble | 97 | 1.4 | 0.4 | 3.9 | 13.1 | 320 |
| Tilapia Tomato Alfredo | 84 | 5.8 | 1.8 | 2.1 | 11.3 | 324 |
| Spicy Halibut Parmesan | 68 | 3.8 | 0.3 | 0.5 | 12.5 | 270 |
| Asian Salmon Meatballs | 99 | 5.6 | 0.5 | 2.5 | 14.2 | 296 |
| Spicy Peanut Salmon Burger | 120 | 7.0 | 0.9 | 3.4 | 16.1 | 477 |
| Asian Ginger catfish | 123 | 3.5 | 1.2 | 1.0 | 12.3 | 518 |
| Cheesy Tuna Mini Casserole | 148 | 12.0 | 4.2 | 3.5 | 18.0 | 670 |
| Mediterranean White Fish | 98 | 3.8 | 1.8 | 1.3 | 14.8 | 340 |
| Garlic Herb Tuna Steak | 95 | 1.3 | 0.2 | 0.8 | 19.7 | 173 |
| Spicy Tuna Cakes | 85 | 4.3 | 0.1 | 3.8 | 8.7 | 312 |
| Balsamic Pork tenderloin | 77 | 2.7 | 0.8 | 1.4 | 15.0 | 550 |
| Pork and Broccoli Stir Fry | 78 | 6.0 | 1.3 | 1.2 | 13.0 | 364 |
| Pork Chop in Mushroom Sauce | 107 | 6.0 | 0.9 | 3.1 | 13.1 | 521 |

| Recipe Name | Calories (kCal) | Carbs (g) | Sugar (g) | Fat (g) | Protein (g) | Sodium (mg) |
|---|---|---|---|---|---|---|
| Pork Chop in Creamy Onion sauce | 95 | 5.5 | 2.8 | 2.4 | 13.6 | 153 |
| Pork Stroganoff | 93 | 7.3 | 2.7 | 1.5 | 13.6 | 448 |
| Vinegar Mustard Glazed Ham Loaf | 146 | 9.6 | 4.3 | 4.7 | 17.3 | 755 |
| Garlic Lemon Scallops | 72 | 5.2 | 0.2 | 0.5 | 11.7 | 450 |
| Scallops in Jalapeno Whisky Cream Sauce | 96 | 7.1 | 1.7 | 0.9 | 12.4 | 623 |
| Lowcountry Shrimps | 75 | 1.2 | 0.4 | 1.6 | 13.5 | 448 |
| Cheesy Onion Scallops | 94 | 6.0 | 0.3 | 0.5 | 12.1 | 460 |
| Shrimp à la Grecque | 97 | 4.3 | 1.7 | 0.9 | 14.1 | 507 |
| Crab Imperial | 76 | 10.8 | 4.9 | 0.6 | 7.4 | 423 |
| Steamed Clams in Garlic Wine Sauce | 168 | 5.7 | 0.1 | 3.6 | 18.9 | 111 |
| Mussels in Marinara Sauce | 174 | 8.1 | 1.3 | 4.9 | 16.9 | 410 |
| Creamy Cajun Shrimps | 69 | 1.2 | 0.4 | 1.3 | 12.7 | 485 |
| Maryland Crab Cake | 69 | 4.1 | 0.6 | 0.7 | 11.5 | 346 |
| Grilled Tomato Basil Marinated Shrimp | 77 | 0.9 | 0.5 | 2.6 | 12.2 | 361 |
| Grilled Lemon Ginger Shrimp | 66 | 1.9 | 0.3 | 1.0 | 12.4 | 345 |
| Taco Salad | 134 | 7.6 | 2.7 | .2.4 | 21.8 | 376 |
| Asian Lettuce Wrap | 121 | 9.0 | 3.5 | 4.1 | 13.0 | 351 |
| Shrimp Salad Stuffed tomatoes | 80 | 4.5 | 2.8 | 1.3 | 12.9 | 309 |
| Sloppy Joe Lettuce Wrap | 82 | 3.6 | 1.6 | 2.2 | 12.8 | 155 |
| Garden Salad with lemon chicken and Feta | 111 | 8.5 | 3.1 | 2.9 | 12.9 | 475 |
| Buffalo Chicken Lettuce Wrap | 92 | 2.0 | 1.0 | 2.1 | 13.1 | 285 |
| Seared Tandoori Tofu | 95 | 3.2 | 0.1 | 4.2 | 7.8 | 239 |
| Italian Portobello Bake | 105 | 14.2 | 1.2 | 1.3 | 11.6 | 393 |
| Baked Garlic Tofu | 102 | 6.6 | 0.3 | 4.7 | 8.9 | 325 |

# THANK YOU FOR READING!

After your bariatric surgery, what you eat play a significant role in healing and nourishing your body.

I hope this book has provide you some new inspiration. Thank you again for picking up my book and going through it.

STELLA LAYNE 2017

Printed in Great Britain
by Amazon